FIRST RESPONDERS

PRACTICAL CAREER GUIDES

Series Editor: Kezia Endsley

Culinary Arts, by Tracy Brown Hamilton
Dental Assistants and Hygienists, by Kezia Endsley
Education Professionals, by Kezia Endsley
First Responders, by Kezia Endsley
Health and Fitness Professionals, by Kezia Endsley
Medical Office Professionals, by Marcia Santore
Skilled Trade Professionals, by Corbin Collins

FIRST RESPONDERS

A Practical Career Guide

KEZIA ENDSLEY

ROWMAN & LITTLEFIELD
Lanham • Boulder • New York • London

Published by Rowman & Littlefield
An imprint of The Rowman & Littlefield Publishing Group, Inc.
4501 Forbes Boulevard, Suite 200, Lanham, Maryland 20706
www.rowman.com

6 Tinworth Street, London, SE11 5AL, United Kingdom

British Library Cataloguing in Publication Information Available

Library of Congress Cataloging-in-Publication Data

Names: Endsley, Kezia, 1968– author.
Title: First responders : a practical career guide / Kezia Endsley.
Description: Lanham : Rowman & Littlefield, [2019] | Series: Practical career guides | Includes bibliographical references.
Identifiers: LCCN 2019016323 (print) | LCCN 2019021936 (ebook) | ISBN 9781538111864 (Electronic) | ISBN 9781538111857 (paperback : alk. paper)
Subjects: LCSH: Emergency management. | First responders. | Vocational guidance.
Classification: LCC HV551.2 (ebook) | LCC HV551.2 .E683 2019 (print) | DDC 363.34/8023—dc23
LC record available at https://lccn.loc.gov/2019016323

∞™ The paper used in this publication meets the minimum requirements of American National Standard for Information Sciences—Permanence of Paper for Printed Library Materials, ANSI/NISO Z39.48-1992.

Contents

Introduction

Careers in the First Responder Fields

*A*re you interested in becoming a firefighter, police officer, emergency medical technician (EMT), or paramedic? If so, you've come to the right source. Welcome to careers in the first responder fields! These are the professions often called first responders and certified first responders. They are trained in various aspects of emergency care and/or emergency response and are often the first ones to arrive at the scene of an accident or crime (hence, first responder). Depending on their area of expertise, they might handle crisis negotiations, extricate someone from a mangled automobile involved in a collision, administer

A career as a first responder can be extremely rewarding.

life-saving emergency medical services to someone in distress, or remove people from burning buildings and administer cardiopulmonary resuscitation (CPR). As you might imagine, these are high-stress and high-reward professions.

There is a lot of good news about these fields, and they are good career choices for anyone with a passion for helping people. They are great careers for people who get energy from helping other people and who can handle stress and pressure well. Demand for these jobs remains high and the job outlook for the next decade is better than the average profession.

When considering any career, your goal should be to find your specific nexus of interest, passion, and job demand. Yes, it is important to consider job outlook and demand, educational requirements, and other such practical matters, but remember that you'll be spending a large portion of your life in whatever career you choose, so you should also find something that you enjoy doing and are passionate about—and this is especially true for first responders. Because of the high demands of these careers, you need to have a passion for your work to avoid burnout and deal with stress.

Of course, it can make the road easier to walk if you choose something that's in demand and stable, like the first responder fields.

A Career as a First Responder

This book covers in detail four main areas in first response. These are:

- Firefighters
- Police officers
- EMTs
- Paramedics and emergency medical professionals

Be sure to check out the Bureau of Labor Statistics website for current US information about these and related professions. You can find specific information about each of these areas on the following pages:

- Firefighters: www.bls.gov/ooh/protective-service/firefighters.htm
- Police officers: www.bls.gov/ooh/protective-service/police-and-detectives .htm
- EMTs, paramedics, and emergency medical professionals: www.bls.gov/ ooh/healthcare/emts-and-paramedics.htm

So what exactly do these people do on the job, day in and day out? What kind of skills, educational background, and certifications do you need to succeed in any of these fields? How much can you expect to make, and what are the pros and cons of these various fields? Do these career paths have a bright future? How do you avoid burnout and deal with stress and tragedy? Is this even the right career path for you? This book can help you answer these questions and more.

> "Being a police officer is a very rewarding job. You're not going to be rich. But it's very fulfilling and satisfying when you can actually help someone."—Lieutenant Mark Ostapowizc, twenty-seven-year veteran police officer

For these professions, the book covers the pros and cons, educational/ training requirements, projected annual wages, personality traits that are well suited, working conditions and expectations, and more. You'll even read some interviews from real professionals working in these fields. The goal is for you to learn enough about these professions to give you a clear view as to which one, if any, is a good fit for you. And if you still have more questions, this book will also point you to resources where you can learn even more.

An important note: Regardless of the career you choose, to succeed in any profession where you work with the public, you need to have a lifelong curiosity and love of learning. Your education won't be over once you finish your training. In fact, maintaining current certifications and meeting or exceeding continuing education requirements (usually set forth by a professional governing board and/or by state regulations where you practice) are very important in careers such as these.

The Market Today

The good news is that the US Bureau of Labor Statistics forecasts that careers in the first response fields are growing as fast or faster than the average marketplace in the current decade. (See www.bls.gov/emp for a full list of employment projections.) The projected change in employment for police officers and firefighters in this country is 7 percent, which matches the average growth rate for all jobs.

For EMTs and paramedics, the projected change is 15 percent, which is much higher than average.[1] First responders will always be necessary, which means you will have job security. New positions are being created in these areas every year as well.

The demand for first response jobs are affected by many factors in the United States:

- We have a large elderly population, as the generation of baby boomers continues to age. This elderly population needs more frequent emergency intervention and care.
- The growing population (young and old) will in general require more emergency and protective services.
- There has been an increase in the number of specialized medical facilities, which corresponds to a need for more EMTs and paramedics to transfer patients with specific conditions to these facilities for treatment.[2]
- There is also a continuous need to replace workers who leave these occupations due to the high stress and the physical demands of these jobs.
- Employment growth for firefighters and police officers (and sometimes EMTs and paramedics) is affected by state and local government budgets and taxes. If a state or local government experiences budget deficits or is unable to increase its tax base, it may be unable to grow these departments as much as it would like. As a result, employment growth may be somewhat reduced in times of economic insecurity.

Chapter 1 covers lots more about the job prospects of these professions, breaking down the numbers for each one into more detail.

What Does This Book Cover?

The goal of this book is to cover all aspects of your search for a career in first response and explain how the professions work and how you can excel in them. Here's a breakdown of the chapters:

- Chapter 1 explains the different careers under the first responder umbrella covered in this book. You'll learn about what people in these professions do in their day-to-day work, the environments in which first responders work, some pros and cons about each career path, the average salaries of these jobs, and the outlook in the future for all these careers.

- Chapter 2 explains in detail the educational and training requirements of these different fields, from medical degrees to certification and academy training. You will learn how to go about getting experience (in the form of shadowing, volunteer work, and explorer programs, for example) in these fields before you enter college as well as during your college years. You'll also learn about the certifications, licensing, and registrations you need (usually set forth by a governing board and/or by regulations in the state where you work) in order to perform these jobs safely and legally.
- Chapter 3 explains all the aspects of college, academy, and postsecondary schooling that you'll want to consider as you move forward. You will learn about the academy training process needed to become a firefighter or police officer, as well as how to get the best education for the best deal. You will also learn a little about scholarships and financial aid and how the SAT and ACT work.
- Chapter 4 covers all aspects of the résumé-writing and interviewing processes, including writing a stellar résumé and cover letter, interviewing to your best potential, dressing for the part, communicating effectively and efficiently, and more.

Where Do You Start?

You can approach the first response field in several different ways—whether you start immediately after high school or pursue a college degree first—depending on your long-term goals and interests. Are you more interested in finding a stable and in-demand position right after high school, or would you rather pursue a degree and work specifically in emergency medicine? Are you more interested in fire safety and prevention and revel at the idea of carrying sixty-five-pound gear around daily, or would you rather help to uphold the law and protect the public in that way?

Regardless of your approach to emergency response, it's important to understand that you will handle stressful, intense, life-and-death situations and will often be dealing with people on the worst day of their lives. Do you have—or can you develop—the mental toughness to deal with these kinds of

Your future awaits!

situations with a level head on a daily basis? This is something important to consider as you shadow and volunteer in various first response environments.

The good news is that you don't need to know the answers to these questions yet. In order to find the best fit for yourself as a first responder, you need to understand how these jobs work. That's where you'll start in chapter 1.

1

Why Choose a Career as a First Responder?

Y ou learned in the introduction that the professions in the first responders field—which includes firefighters, police officers, emergency medical technician (EMTs), and paramedics—are healthy and growing. You also learned a little bit about the demands and mental stresses of these professions. And you were reminded that it's important to pursue a career that you enjoy, are good at, and are passionate about. You will spend a lot of your life working; it makes sense to find something you enjoy doing. Of course, you want to make money and support yourself while doing it. If you love the idea of helping people for a living, you've come to the right book.

This chapter breaks out these professions and covers the basics of each. The nice thing is that no matter what kind of training, postsecondary education, or degree you can or want to pursue, there is a way for you to work in emergency response. College isn't for everybody. Not everyone wants to—or can afford to—spend four or more years at a university taking academic classes in order to find a good job.

More than 50 percent of college students who start at a four-year institution drop out by year six of their college career.[1] An overwhelming majority of those students leave college with substantial student loan debt.

However, even though you might not need a college education, you do still need to finish high school, pursue a technical degree and certifications, and probably also attend academy. This training can take anywhere from six months to two years.

The role of an emergency physician also fits under the emergency medical service umbrella, but it's not covered in detail in this book, as it requires a full medical degree and board certification in emergency medical services. If you're specifically interested in being an emergency physician, you can start by checking out the American College of Emergency Physicians website at www.acep.org and the American Academy of Emergency Medicine website at www.aaem.org.

After reading this chapter, you should have a good understanding of each of these careers and can then start to determine if one of them is a good fit for you. Let's start with the venerable firefighter.

What Do Firefighters Do?

We all know that a big part of any firefighter's job is to control and put out fires, but they also routinely respond to emergencies in which lives, property, or the environment are at risk. They enter burning buildings to rescue people and put out fires, provide medical services and first aid, and work with hazardous materials. In addition, a big part of their job is educating the public about fire safety in order to prevent fires.

In the case of an accident that does not involve a fire (such as an automobile accident), firefighters use their EMT training to care for the injured and secure the scene before paramedics and police arrive. They also act as rescuers in the case of natural disasters such as tornadoes, tsunamis, and earthquakes. Firefighters treat the victims of these disasters and search for the missing.

Two out of three calls to firefighters are for medical emergencies, not fires, according to the National Fire Protection Association.[2] By that same token, the majority of firefighters these days are also certified EMTs, and many are further certified as paramedics.

The typical day-to-day responsibilities of a firefighter range from mundane to potentially life-altering:

- Cleaning, inspecting, and maintaining equipment
- Conducting and participating in drills and physical fitness trainings
- Driving fire trucks and other emergency vehicles

In addition to rescue, many firefighters provide medical attention and first aid to people in need.

- Putting out fires using water hoses, fire extinguishers, and water pumps
- Finding and rescuing victims in burning structures or in other emergency situations
- Treating injured people
- Preparing written reports on emergency incidents
- Investigating the sources of fires
- Performing business inspections to ensure adherence to local fire codes
- Educating the public about fire safety[3]

In addition, some firefighters are specially trained to control and clean up hazardous materials.

As you might imagine, the state of California has the highest employment level per thousand firefighters in the nation and has the second-highest average wage for firefighters (after New York). A special need in California is for wildland firefighters, who are specially trained to use heavy equipment and water hoses to control forest fires.[4]

When firefighters are not responding to a call, they are on-site at the fire station. They eat and sleep at the station while they remain on call, and their shifts usually last twenty-four hours. During this downtime, they may clean and inspect equipment, work out and exercise, attend trainings and renew certifications, provide education and outreach to the community, and socialize and dine with their fellow firefighters.

In addition to staying in excellent physical shape, firefighters must be involved in ongoing education and regular drills and training. Additional specialty areas that some firefighters pursue include:

- Handling hazardous materials
- Wildland firefighting
- Water and underground rescues
- EMT certifications
- Fire and arson investigations
- Inspections and fire codes

Although a career as a firefighter doesn't typically require any formal education beyond a high school diploma or general equivalency diploma (GED), having some secondary education classes or an associate's degree in fire science can give you a leg up against the stiff competition and lead to additional opportunities. Regardless of your educational experience, the main part of your training takes place on the job. You will be expected to pass written, physical, and medical examinations before being considered for a job opening.

Once you are hired as a new recruit, you'll participate in rigorous physical training exercises and classroom work at the academy before you can enter the field. Nearly all firefighters in the United States must be certified as EMTs before being allowed in the field, but this depends on the city or municipality.[5] EMT training can take up to one year and results in EMT-Basic certification. More information about the EMT process and profession is found later in this chapter.

Most firefighters work some version of the Kelly shift schedule, which involves working three twenty-four-hour shifts on alternate days, followed by four consecutive days off. You might work on Wednesday, Friday, and Sunday, and then have the next four days off. This type of schedule rotates, so you would then work twenty-four-hour shifts on Friday, Sunday, and Tuesday, and then be off the next four days.

This is just an overview—chapters 2 and 3 cover the educational and professional certification requirements to become a firefighter in more detail.

THE VOLUNTEER FIRE DEPARTMENT MODEL

According to the National Fire Protection Association, two-thirds of firefighters in the United States are volunteers.[6] If you include fire stations that are characterized as "mostly volunteer," nearly 85 percent of US fire departments are in some way manned by volunteer firefighters. What does this mean for you as a potential firefighter?

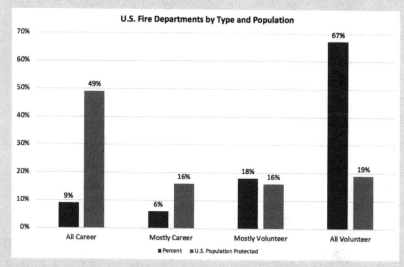

The volunteer firefighter is by far the most common in the United States. *NFPA, Research, Data & Analytics. NFPA, 1 Batterymarch Park, Quincy, MA 02169, www.nfpa.org*

Being a volunteer firefighter requires hundreds of hours of training and a dedication to public service. Not all departments have volunteers, and depending upon your area, volunteer opportunities may not be available. Factors like population and local government policies determine the structure of a city's fire department.

If you're looking for information about volunteering, the best first step is to call your local fire station's nonemergency number and ask to speak with the station officer. Tell him or her that you're interested in becoming a volunteer and ask what your next step should be. He or she should be able to direct you to the best resources. If you're over eighteen, departments will often allow you to ride along on their apparatus so you can make a more informed decision about whether volunteer firefighting is right for you. Many volunteer departments also require a minimum number of hours per month, so don't be afraid to ask about required hours as well.

After you join, the department will usually enter you into an intensive training program. These programs vary in length, but all firefighters are required to take a minimum 110-hour National Fire Protection Association–certified course.

Volunteer firefighters do not get paid, but they sometimes do get reimbursed. Reimbursement is usually a small amount of tax-free money for time spent on shifts, responding to calls, and training. Volunteering is one of the best ways to get the necessary training and experience to be an excellent candidate for a career firefighting position. As towns and cities grow, they typically need to have full-time paid staff—career firefighters, in other words. If you've been a volunteer firefighter, you are in a great position to qualify for those new career positions.

If your local department doesn't have volunteers, check nearby towns and departments. FEMA (https://apps.usfa.fema.gov/registry/) has a national fire department registry and is a good place to start.

THE PROS AND CONS OF BEING A FIREFIGHTER

The good news is that firefighting is a stable and in-demand job. The job growth rate for firefighters is on par with the national average, which you'll read more about in a later section. In addition, the pay is pretty good, especially when you consider it does not require an advanced degree. However, most firefighters don't enter the profession for its job security or pay. They are drawn to firefighting for the opportunity to help people, often risking their own lives to do so.

One of the major advantages that firefighters mention (after being able to help people) is the camaraderie. Firefighters often develop tight bonds and friendships among themselves because they come to rely on each other in life-and-death situations. The relationships built at the fire station can be fun, intense, and lifelong. Many firefighters refer to it as the brother/sisterhood.

Because you truly do not know what emergency situations will be coming your way each day, the day-to-day environment and challenges can vary greatly. Being a firefighter never gets mundane or boring. Each shift is a new, exciting experience. In addition, the twenty-four-hour shifts afford firefighters multiple days off in a row and a flexible schedule during their off days.

If helping people and being a part of a team are motivators for you, being a firefighter may just be the right fit.

> Firefighters overwhelmingly report that being a part of a team of firefighters is one of the best aspects of their job. If you don't enjoy or can't fathom working on a team and depending on others for help and to keep you safe, this is not the profession for you.

Despite its many advantages, there are a few cons to consider as well. One issue to keep in mind is the physicality of the job. The firefighting profession requires you to be in top physical shape. The stamina and strength needed to climb ladders, carry heavy hoses, break down doors, operate pumps, set up hydraulic jacks, and open fire hydrants is not insignificant. The gear that firefighters wear on their bodies weighs in excess of sixty-five pounds. Due to these physical demands, most firefighters retire and take their pensions sometime in their fifties.

It should come as no surprise that this also can be a dangerous profession. Exhaustion, dehydration, smoke inhalation, and muscle strain can occur, especially when a rash of fires breaks out. Firefighters may be injured when handling emergency situations, such as extricating an accident victim from a mangled car along a busy freeway. In addition, today's fires are made up of burning plastics and therefore produce toxic flames. These environments have been correlated with higher incidence of many kinds of cancers in firefighters.

CANCER AND THE FIREFIGHTER

In a 2013 study of thirty thousand firefighters from three large cities (Chicago, Philadelphia, and San Francisco), researchers from the National Institute for Occupational Safety and Health (NIOSH) found that:

- Cancers of the respiratory, digestive, and urinary systems primarily accounted for the higher rates of cancer in firefighters.
- The population of firefighters in the study had a rate of mesothelioma (a type of cancer that affects the thin layer of tissue that covers many organs)

two times greater than the rate in the US population. This was the first study ever to identify a higher rate of mesothelioma in US firefighters. This is likely associated with exposure to asbestos, a known cause of mesothelioma.[7]

These findings are generally consistent with the results of several previous, smaller studies. Because this study had a larger population that was followed for a longer period of time, the results strengthen the scientific evidence for a relationship between firefighting and cancer.

Firefighters are exposed to contaminants from fires that are known or suspected to cause cancer. These include combustion by-products such as benzene and form-aldehyde, and materials such as asbestos from older buildings and other structures.

The good news is that modern fire departments are taking these risks very seriously and mitigating them by providing firefighters with advanced protective gear and ensuring that all gear is cleaned and free from contaminants, and attempting to reduce these cancer risks by following newer, enhanced safety procedures.

Another issue that is more recently being talked about and addressed is the emotional trauma and post-traumatic stress disorder (PTSD) that is an occupational hazard for first responders. Unresolved issues about things they have witnessed and people they could not save can lead to emotional and substance abuse issues.[8] Thankfully, more and more fire departments are taking such issues seriously and helping firefighters get the help they need. Many firefighters say that having a sound, healthy mind and good coping skills is a requirement for anyone considering the profession, as is the willingness to reach out for help to deal with these kinds of situations.

"The hardest part [of being a firefighter] is the mental strain. I've seen lots of things that I wish I could unsee. It's hard to leave it all at work, for sure. Being diagnosed with PTSD is common for firefighters. You have to process it and talk to someone about it, preferably a professional. Validation from senior firefighters can really help as well. You need to talk to someone."—Matt Hahn, twenty-year veteran firefighter

HOW HEALTHY IS THE JOB MARKET FOR FIREFIGHTERS?

The Bureau of Labor Statistics is part of the US Department of Labor. It tracks statistical information about thousands of careers in the United States. For anyone wanting to become a firefighter, the news is good. Employment is expected to grow 7 percent in the decade from 2016 to 2026, which is as fast as the national average.

These statistics show just how promising this career is now and in the foreseeable future:

- *Education:* Most firefighters need a high school diploma and some training in emergency medical services (EMSs). Most departments require their firefighters to be EMTs; they often provide that training and certification to new recruits. However, prior certification as an EMT and classes or a degree in fire science can set you apart from other potential recruits.
- *Training:* New recruits attend a twelve-week-long fire academy school, usually run by the fire department or the state. This process includes classroom instruction and practical training, during which trainees learn how to fight fires with standard equipment, including axes, chainsaws, fire extinguishers, and ladders.
- *2017 median pay:* $49,080
- *Job outlook 2016–2026:* 7 percent (as fast as the national average)
- *Work environment:* Most (90 percent) work under the jurisdiction of local governments; many departments (a full 85 percent) are run by volunteer firefighters.[9]

In addition to this training and education, you must be at least eighteen years of age, be a citizen of the United States, and have no felonies to work as a firefighter; many departments and states require a minimum age of twenty-one. To increase your odds, be physically fit and have an EMT—or even better, a paramedic certification.

THE PARAMEDIC FIREFIGHTER EXPERIENCE

Michael McNeely.
Courtesy of Michael McNeely

Michael McNeely is a lieutenant firefighter and paramedic for the fire department in Carmel, Indiana, a city outside Indianapolis with about ninety thousand residents. He also serves as a public information officer (marketing and social media) for the department. He has been with the Carmel Fire Department since 2005.

Can you explain how you became interested in being a paramedic and firefighter, and talk about your career path a bit?

When I was five or six years old, my mom took me to our local station. The firefighters took the time to show me the trucks and show me around. I loved it. I knew then I wanted to be a firefighter, and I never grew out of that idea. I started volunteering and got into some explorer programs for teens. When I was old enough (twenty-one years old), I started applying to departments all over the country—from Michigan to Florida. I've been with the Carmel Fire Department for fourteen years. I worked for a small department in Tennessee briefly before joining Carmel FD. I also worked in the ER as a paramedic for five years.

What are your main job duties, and how does your department serve the community?

There are 160 firefighters in Carmel, and they are all EMTs as well. A handful also become paramedics—they are advanced in the medical field. They can do more than nurses can.

Our trucks combined go out the door about seventeen thousand times on emergency calls. We could have twelve to fifteen runs in a shift (twenty-four hours). We also inspect buildings and educate the public, all in a day.

We are a very busy department and are very progressive—we are always looking for the next best thing, whether it's equipment, thermal cameras on helmets, technology, education, or training. We are fortunate to have adequate funding and good support from the public.

About 60 to 70 percent of our runs are medical emergencies. Carmel has one paramedic on each fire engine and each ambulance. There is one fire engine at each station and four ambulances that rotate, and then one ladder truck.

As a paramedic, every morning I check the truck as well as the meds and supplies onboard to make sure everything is fully stocked and the equipment is in good standing. There are also a lot of training hours to keep your paramedic license. It's a yearly license and involves either online work or going to classes.

If we get a run, we have ninety seconds to be on the truck and out the door. If it's a medical run, the paramedics are the leaders and orchestrate things. The EMTs are the helpers and the workers. The paramedic coordinates the whole scene. Paramedics take patients to the hospital, talk to the doctors there, and are responsible for filling out lengthy legal documents afterward. You must document everything that happened.

What is your formal educational background?

I went to college for mechanical engineering, but I didn't want to work in an office. This gave me a good working knowledge of how things were built. I knew I didn't want to work at a desk. I went through EMT school, which gave me medical knowledge. I enjoyed that, which further showed me that I would enjoy being a firefighter.

As many as six hundred people take the general knowledge test. The top two hundred people will be offered interviews. We then take the top recruits and send them through recruit school (hazmat, etc.) for six to eight months. It's Monday-to-Friday training, book work in the morning, physical activities in the afternoon. Then it's probationary for one year. After that point, they become "true" firefighters.

What drew you to being a paramedic?

After going on so many runs without being a paramedic, I realized I wanted to be the one calling the shots, giving the medications, and saving the lives. I was a firefighter/EMT for two years, then I went to paramedic school (two years), which involved classroom and clinical work. I was still working as a firefighter during that time as well.

What's the best part of being a paramedic/firefighter?

We help people. We show up and fix problems and save lives, or we can quickly get them help elsewhere. No day is ever the same. You don't know what to expect from day to day.

What is the most surprising thing about your job?

The amount of work and obligations that our department has. It's not just fires—it's so much more than that. That includes building inspections (two thousand buildings yearly here), new home building inspections, kids' camps, visiting schools to talk to kids, and general outreach with the community.

What are some of the challenges of being a paramedic?

The medical field changes often, all based on new scientific information. So you have to stay up on the latest training, which is a challenge. The amount of time away from your family is also hard.

What would be your dream job within this field?

Doing what I am doing—which is getting on the truck every time the bell rings to help someone.

What are some characteristics of a good first responder? What people really don't fit well in this field?

You need to be honest, get along well with others, fit well with groups, be physically fit and enjoy fitness, think on the fly, and be able to listen and take orders from others.

People with tragic events in the lives can have a hard time dealing with the seriousness of the job. You need to be emotionally and mentally stable.

What are some of the challenges facing EMTs these days?

Across the nation, it's budget issues. The pay is often subpar, and this is often where the cuts come. The hours are long, and time away from family is difficult. It's not worth it if you don't love helping people.

The twenty-four-hour shifts away from your family are hard. Weekends and holidays, we are here. That's a stress.

It's dangerous, too. As many as 60 percent of retired firefighters have some form of cancer. No more dirty gear—it's not a badge of experience anymore; it's dangerous.

What advice do you have for young people considering a career as a paramedic? As a firefighter?

Number one—stay out of trouble. They will kick you out of the process for very little anymore. You have to be smart and do well in school now, especially with the EMT/paramedic portion. Do your best in school.

How can a young person prepare for this career while in high school?

Getting involved in volunteer or explorer programs. Make physical fitness a priority. Start trying out when you are nineteen. Get your EMT and then paramedic license. We really need paramedics. That's your way in. Some states you can be eighteen to be a firefighter, but most require a minimum of age twenty-one.

WOULD I BE A GOOD FIREFIGHTER?

Ask yourself these questions:

- Do I have a servant's heart—am I driven to help and serve people?
- Am I a team player and truly enjoy being part of a team?
- Can I keep my cool in stressful and traumatic situations?
- I am physically fit or willing to get there? Do I enjoy working out and being active?
- Can I be compassionate, understanding, and nonjudgmental, no matter who I am treating?
- Do I have a sound, healthy mind and good coping skills?
- Am I ready and willing to treat people medically and learn the skills to be an EMT?
- Am I a lifelong learner and excited at the prospect of continuously learning?

> "As a firefighter, you need a willingness to never stop learning! It's really changed in the fifteen years since I've been one. Yes, it's essentially still 'put the wet stuff on the red stuff,' but the techniques, equipment, dangers, etc., have all changed significantly."—Tim Griffin, fifteen-year veteran firefighter

If the answer to any of these questions is an adamant *no*, you might want to consider a different path. Remember that learning what you *don't* like can be just as important as figuring out what you *do* like. If you still aren't sure whether fire services is your gig, read on to learn about what it takes to be a police officer.

What Do Police Officers Do?

You probably don't need a career book to tell you what a police officer is. Police officers are ubiquitous in our country—every city, county, and state has a law enforcement department. But you may not realize how much police officers do in addition to day-to-day law enforcement.

A police officer can wear many hats during the course of his or her career. Your range of responsibilities will depend on the size of the department and on the population that you serve, but they often include the following:

- Patrolling areas for criminal activity and victim assistance
- Collecting and securing evidence from crime scenes
- Conducting traffic stops and issuing citations
- Observing the activities of suspects
- Responding to emergency and nonemergency calls
- Obtaining warrants and arrest suspects
- Writing detailed reports and filling out forms
- Preparing cases and testifying in court
- Interacting with the public in educational and nonenforcement capacities[10]

Police officers can work in a variety of settings, including for local and state governments, for the federal government, as detectives and criminal investigators, and even as fish and game wardens. Every midsized or larger department has officers who specialize in SWAT, vice, internal affairs, community outreach, detective work, education through Youth Explorer programs and camps, general patrol, and more.

- *Patrol unit:* These officers are the most essential and basic part of the force, and patrol work takes up the majority of police time. These are the officers out on the beat, patrolling their assigned areas. They do traffic stops, check for warrants, and make arrests.
- *SWAT unit:* The SWAT (Special Weapons and Tactics) team is an elite unit that is used in exceptional crisis situations that require increased firepower or special tactics. They often deal with hostage and terrorist situations, for example.
- *Vice unit:* These officers focus on crime related to narcotics, alcohol, gambling, and prostitution. These officers sometimes go undercover to investigate potential illegal operations.
- *Internal affairs unit:* These officers investigate and unearth what really occurred when an officer or department is accused of misconduct. They typically work outside of the traditional command structure.
- *Detective unit:* These officers gather facts and collect evidence for criminal cases, conducting interviews, examining records, observing the

activities of suspects, and participating in raids and arrests. Detectives usually specialize in investigating one type of crime, such as homicide or fraud. They can be uniformed or plainclothes investigators.

• *Community outreach and education unit:* These officers work with and educate the community about local law enforcement by visiting schools, giving tours, and holding and attending local events, with the goal of strengthening relationships with the community they serve. They engage with the community in positive, nonenforcement situations to strengthen relationships and build trust within the community.

"[To be a good police officer], you must like to help people. You have to care about people and want to help them. People call you at their worst. It's crisis time and they want your help."—Mark Ostapowicz, twenty-seven-year veteran police officer

If you want to be a police officer or detective, you need at least a high school diploma or equivalent. In addition, many federal agencies and some local and state police departments require some college coursework or even a college degree. Many community colleges, four-year colleges, and universities have programs in law enforcement and criminal justice, which can give you a leg up during the recruitment process.

Chapters 2 and 3 cover the educational and professional certification requirements to become a police officer in more detail.

THE PROS AND CONS OF BEING A POLICE OFFICER

The good news is that law enforcement is a stable and in-demand job. The job growth rate for law enforcement is on par with the national average, which you'll read more about in a later section. The number of recruits entering general law enforcement is low all over the country right now, which means it's a good time to get into law enforcement if it's your calling.

As described previously, law enforcement includes many areas of specialization, which means you can find the area/unit that interests you the most; you can also move around during the span of your career for variety. Camaraderie

Being a police officer can be extremely rewarding when you're able to help someone in real distress.

with other officers and with the department in general is also one pro that many in law enforcement state as a real benefit of the job. Much like the firefighters, a real bond—like a family—develops over time with fellow officers. In addition, the pay and benefits are pretty good, especially when you consider it does not require an advanced degree. However, most police officers don't enter the profession for its job security or pay. They are drawn to law enforcement, like all first responders, because they want to serve the public and help people.

Because you do not know what situations will be coming your way each day, the day-to-day environment and challenges can vary greatly. Being a police officer never gets mundane or boring. Each shift is a new, exciting experience. In addition, the twenty-four-hour shifts afford officers multiple days off in a row and a flexible schedule during their off days.

Despite its many advantages, there are a few cons to consider as well. For one, it's a physically demanding job, and it can be stressful and dangerous. You could very well be put in harm's way. Officers can be injured when handling emergency situations. In addition, you will likely work weekends and holidays. Another drawback includes the amount of paperwork the job involves, which can be off-putting to some.

CAN YOU BE PART OF THE SOLUTION?

As a profession, law enforcement has suffered many public relations blows in the past years. Because the media is much more likely to report on the bad incidents than on the good, police officers are often seen as uncaring, racist, and jaded—and indeed, some of them are. This negative attention that law enforcement is getting from the media—that they are all racist and uncaring—has seriously curtailed the recruiting process. People see only the bad and not the good that police departments do every day.

This is greatly affecting how many young people want to go into law enforcement. This is a problem nationwide. There are alarmingly low numbers of potential recruits in police academies all over the country. But what you might not realize is that many departments are making a serious effort to confront and address these problems.

How do we fix community-police relations as a country? It's not something we can do in a year—it has to be forever. Young people who care about these issues, who have a passion to make things better, are the key to repairing and strengthening community relationships—which in turn will help with recruitment.

Are you one of those young people?

HOW HEALTHY IS THE JOB MARKET FOR LAW ENFORCEMENT?

The Bureau of Labor Statistics tracks statistical information about thousands of careers in the United States. For anyone wanting to become a police officer, the news is good. Employment is expected to grow 7 percent in the decade from 2016 to 2026, which is as fast as the national average. Demand is steady and the supply of recruits is at a national low, as discussed in the sidebar "Can You Be Part of the Solution?"

These statistics show just how promising this career is now and in the foreseeable future:

- *Education:* Requirements range from a high school diploma to a college degree. Check with your local and state agencies for their specific qualifications.
- *Training:* Recruits must graduate from their agency's training academy before completing a period of on-the-job training.

- *2017 median pay:* $62,960
- *Job outlook 2016–2026:* 7 percent (as fast as the national average)
- *Work environment:* The majority (89 percent) work for state or local agencies, with another 7 percent working for federal agencies.[11]

In addition to this training and education, you usually must be at least twenty-one years of age, be a citizen of the United States, and have no felonies to work as a police officer. You must also meet stringent physical and personal qualifications. To increase your odds, be physically fit and have some postsecondary coursework in law enforcement or criminal justice.

FEDERAL LAW ENFORCEMENT OPTIONS

The federal government has created myriad agencies to help detect, investigate, prevent, and apprehend offenders who commit federal crimes. Due to the wide range of crimes under the federal umbrella, each agency has distinct and well-defined responsibilities. The requirements and qualifications for these agencies vary greatly as well. You can visit the following websites for more information if you're interested in any of these areas of federal law enforcement:

- Bureau of Alcohol, Tobacco, Firearms and Explosives (ATF): www.atf.gov
- Central Intelligence Agency (CIA): www.cia.gov
- Department of Homeland Security: www.dhs.gov
- Drug Enforcement Administration (DEA): www.dea.gov
- Federal Bureau of Investigations (FBI): www.fbi.gov
- Federal Emergency Management Agency (FEMA): www.fema.gov
- IRS Criminal Investigation: www.irs.gov
- Secret Service: www.secretservice.gov
- Transportation Security Administration (TSA): www.tsa.gov
- US Coast Guard: www.uscg.mil

If you are interested specifically in federal law enforcement, there are many more agencies besides these as well. To find out more, start by searching the internet and visiting the federal agency sites.

WOULD I BE A GOOD POLICE OFFICER?

Ask yourself these questions:

- Do I have a servant's heart—am I driven to help and serve people?
- Can I keep my cool in stressful and traumatic situations?
- I am physically fit or willing to get there? Do I enjoy working out and being active?
- Can I be compassionate, understanding, and nonjudgmental, no matter who I am interacting with?
- Do I have a sound, healthy mind and good coping skills?
- Am I a good communicator and ready and willing to communicate with all kinds of different people?
- Am I a lifelong learner and excited at the prospect of continuously learning?

If the answer to any of these questions is an adamant *no*, you might want to consider a different path. Remember that learning what you *don't* like can be just as important as figuring out what you *do* like. If you still aren't sure whether law enforcement is your gig but are drawn to the life of a first responder, read on to learn about what it takes to work in emergency services.

What Do EMTs Do?

EMTs work in the EMS profession. They are specifically trained and certified to treat the sick and injured in emergency situations. EMTs respond to emergency 911 calls by performing medical services as they are transporting patients to medical facilities. They are often the first ones at the scene of an accident or injury. Recall that most firefighters in this country are required to be certified EMTs. However, you can be an EMT and not be a firefighter. (The paramedic requires additional medical training beyond the EMT and is discussed in the following section.)

EMT duties include any of the following, which are often done in coordination with law enforcement officers and firefighters:

- Responding to 911 calls by providing emergency medical assistance
- Providing first aid treatment or life support care to sick or injured patients

- Transferring patients in an ambulance to the emergency department of a hospital or other healthcare facility
- Reporting their observations and treatment to physicians, nurses, or other healthcare facility staff at the facility
- Documenting medical care given to patients
- Taking inventory, replacing, and cleaning supplies, and equipment after use[12]

EMTs often work for independent ambulance services companies, but they also may be employed by state, local, or private hospital organizations or local governments in coordination with the local fire department.

There are three levels of EMT certification: EMT-Basic (EMT-B), EMT-Intermediate (EMT-I), and EMT-Paramedic. EMT-B certification is the entry-level EMT certification, and the courses train students in basic EMT skills. EMT-I certification is the next step in EMT certification. EMT-I certification courses train students in more complicated procedures. In most states, EMT-B certification must be obtained before enrolling in an EMT-I course, because the intermediate course builds on skills learned in the basic course.[13]

Because the exact regulations and requirements vary from state to state, it's smart to obtain your EMT certification in the state in which you plan to practice or in a state with stricter regulations. Chapter 3 covers much more about the education and training needed to become an EMT.

You may have also heard of emergency medical responders (EMRs). These are people trained to provide basic medical care with minimal equipment. They may provide immediate lifesaving interventions while waiting for other EMS resources to arrive. Jobs in this category may also go by a variety of titles, including emergency care attendants, certified first responders, or similar.[14]

THE PROS AND CONS OF BEING AN EMT

The good news is that EMTs are in demand. The job growth rate for EMTs is much higher than the national average, which you'll read more about in a later section.

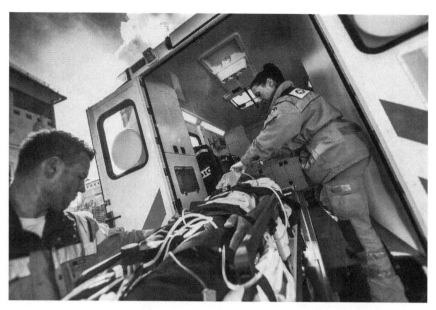

EMTs are often the first at the scene and are responsible for safely transporting patients to medical facilities.

Being an EMT can be an extremely rewarding profession, as you get a chance to save lives literally every time you're on the job. But with that incredible responsibility comes lots of stress and trauma. You will see people on what is possibly the worst day of their lives, and you often see all the worst aspects of human nature. Just like with firefighters and police officers, the day-to-day environment fluctuates and is never boring. Each shift is a new, exciting experience, with a chance to learn new skills constantly.

Despite its many advantages and the great personal reward, there are a few cons to consider as well. For one, it should come as no surprise that this can be a dangerous profession. EMTs (and paramedics) have one of the highest rates of injury and illness of all occupations. They must do considerable kneeling, bending, and lifting while caring for and moving patients. They are often exposed to contagious diseases and viruses, such as hepatitis and HIV. Sometimes they can be injured by difficult or incoherent patients. You can reduce these risks by following proper safety procedures, such as waiting for police to clear an area in violent situations or wearing gloves while working with patients.

As with other first responders, EMTs are also at a higher risk for emotional trauma and PTSD. Unresolved issues with things they have witnessed and people they could not save can lead to emotional and substance abuse issues. You'll need to talk to someone and reach out for help to deal with these situations.

Consider the following characteristics of the EMT career. What might be a disadvantage to some is an advantage to another, so it's a good idea to know what you want and need out of a career as you learn and read about each profession.

- *High reward:* The job you do can literally save lives.
- *Team setting:* You work as a team with other first responders, which can be very rewarding and builds tight bonds with others.
- *Job security:* With the baby boomer population growing older, there will be a continued and increasing demand for emergency services.
- *Physically demanding:* As with other first responder jobs, this is a job that requires a lot of physical stamina to do well.
- *Good career foundation:* Many medical and nursing students, as well as future firefighters, use the experience and skills gained as an EMT as a foundation for more lucrative careers.

HOW HEALTHY IS THE JOB MARKET FOR EMTS?

The Bureau of Labor Statistics tracks statistical information about thousands of careers in the United States. For anyone wanting to become an EMT, the news is great! Employment is expected to grow 15 percent in the decade from 2016 to 2026, which is faster than average. Job demand is healthy due to an increasing elderly population that requires more services and the changing nature of healthcare in the United States.

These statistics show just how promising this career is now and in the foreseeable future:

- *Education:* A high school diploma or equivalent and cardiopulmonary resuscitation (CPR) certification are usually required to begin a postsecondary educational program in emergency medical technology. Most of these programs are nondegree award programs that can be completed in less than one year; some last up to two years.
- *2017 median pay:* $34,280
- *Job outlook 2016–2026:* 13 percent (faster than the national average)

- *Work environment:* The majority work for independent ambulance services companies, but may be employed by state, local, or private hospital organizations or local governments. [15]

WOULD I BE A GOOD EMT?

Ask yourself these questions:

- Am I ready and willing to treat people medically and learn the skills to be an EMT?
- Can I keep my cool in stressful and traumatic—even life-and-death—situations?
- Am I a team player and truly enjoy being part of a team?
- Can I be compassionate, understanding, and nonjudgmental, no matter who I am treating?
- Do I have a sound, healthy mind and good coping skills?
- Am I a lifelong learner and excited at the prospect of continuously learning?
- Am I a good listener and communicator?

If the answer to any of these questions is an adamant *no*, you might want to consider a different path. Remember that learning what you *don't* like can be just as important as figuring out what you *do* like. If you feel driven to be a first responder in some capacity, there are myriad other choices you can pick from.

What Do Paramedics Do?

The EMT-Paramedic (EMT-P) is the highest level of EMT certification. To begin an EMT-P course, you typically need to have completed both your EMT-B and EMT-I certifications. Then you will complete about two additional years of training, which includes classwork, lab work, and fieldwork. EMT-P certification courses focus on the more advanced practice of medicine, like pharmacology, cardiology, and anatomy. To receive EMT-P certification, you usually have to complete an internship working in a hospital or ambulance. [16]

Paramedics perform more advanced medical procedures than EMTs do, including administering medications orally and intravenously, starting intravenous lines, providing advanced airway management for patients, interpreting electrocardiograms, and learning to resuscitate and support patients with significant health problems such as heart attacks and traumas.

In fact, the scope of practice differences between EMTs and paramedics can essentially be summed up by the ability to break the skin. Most states do not allow basic EMTs to give shots or start intravenous lifelines. Paramedics, on the other hand, can give shots as well as use more advanced airway management devices to support breathing. Paramedics are trained in the use of between thirty and forty medications, depending on the state.[17]

If you are interested in becoming a firefighter in a very competitive area, becoming a paramedic is one way to make yourself more appealing to local fire departments. Most fire departments need paramedics on staff, and they are generally harder to come by.

THE PROS AND CONS OF BEING A PARAMEDIC

The pros and cons of being a paramedic are essentially the same as those involved with being an EMT. It's an extremely rewarding job that is in high demand at the moment, but it's also a very high-stress and physical job. Being a paramedic means that you make the decisions, call the shots, and push the meds on the scene, so the pressure and burden of responsibility can feel even heavier. Make sure you are the kind of person who can maintain a cool head in stressful situations and make good decisions when the chips are down.

See the pros and cons section covering EMTs, earlier in this chapter, for more pros and cons that also apply to working as a paramedic.

HOW HEALTHY IS THE JOB MARKET FOR PARAMEDICS?

The Bureau of Labor Statistics tracks statistical information about thousands of careers in the United States. For anyone wanting to become a paramedic, the news is great! Employment is expected to grow 15 percent in the decade from 2016 to 2026, which is faster than the national average. As mentioned previously, job demand is healthy due to an increasing elderly population that requires more services and due to the changing nature of healthcare in this country.

These statistics show just how promising this career is now and in the foreseeable future:

- *Education:* To enter a paramedical training program, you must already be EMT certified. The paramedical training program requires about twelve hundred additional hours of instruction and may lead to an associate's or bachelor's degree.
- *2017 median pay:* $33,380
- *Job outlook 2016–2026:* 15 percent (faster than the national average)
- *Work environment:* The majority work for independent ambulance services companies, but may be employed by state, local, or private hospital organizations or local governments.[18]

WOULD I BE A GOOD PARAMEDIC?

Ask yourself these questions, which are very similar to the EMT-related questions:

- Am I ready and willing to treat people medically and learn the skills to be in emergency medicine?
- Am I willing to be a leader among other emergency services personnel and make the decisions for treatment on the scene of a call?
- Can I keep my cool in stressful and traumatic—even life-and-death—situations?
- Am I a team player and truly enjoy being part of a team?
- Am I a good listener and communicator?
- Can I be compassionate, understanding, and nonjudgmental, no matter who I am treating?
- Do I have a sound, healthy mind and good coping skills?
- Am I a lifelong learner and excited at the prospect of continuously learning?

If the answer to any of these questions is an adamant *no,* you might want to consider a different path. Remember that learning what you *don't* like can be just as important as figuring out what you *do* like. If you're a high school student and wondering whether you are fit to be an EMT or paramedic, be sure to take courses in anatomy and physiology and consider becoming certified in CPR. These courses will help you determine if you enjoy medicine.

Summary

In this chapter, you learned a lot about the different careers under the first responders umbrella—firefighters, police officers, EMTs, and paramedics. You've learned about what people in these professions do in their day-to-day work, the environments where you can find these people working, some pros and cons about each career path, the average salaries of these jobs, and the outlook in the future for all these careers. You hopefully even contemplated some questions about whether your personal likes, career goals, and preferences meld well with these callings. At this time, you should have a good idea about what each job looks like. Are you starting to get excited about one career choice over another? If not, that's okay, as there's still time.

An important takeaway from this chapter is that no matter which of these professions you might pursue, a real desire to help people should be at the forefront of your mind if you want to be successful in any first responder field. The risks, stresses, and challenges of these professions won't likely be worth it to you if you aren't ultimately driven to help people. You need a "servant's heart," as they say, to be a first responder.

Chapter 2 dives into forming a plan for your future, covering everything there is to know about educational requirements, certifications, training courses, and more, about each of these careers. You'll learn about finding summer jobs and making the most of volunteer work as well. The goal is for you to set yourself apart—and above—the rest.

2

Forming a Career Plan

Now that you have some idea what these first responder careers are all about—and maybe you even know which type of emergency response you are interested in—it's time to formulate a career plan. For you organized folks out there, this can be a helpful and energizing process. If you're not a naturally organized person, or if the idea of looking ahead and building a plan to adulthood scares you, you are not alone. That's what this chapter is for.

After discussing ways to develop a career plan—there is more than one way to do this!—the chapter dives into the various requirements. Finally, it will look at how you can gain experience in the field through explorer programs, camps, shadowing, ride-alongs, certifications, and more. Yes, experience will look good on your résumé, and in some cases it's even required, but even more important, getting out there and seeing what first responders do every day is the best way to determine if it's really something that you will enjoy. When you find a career that you truly enjoy and have a passion for, it will rarely feel like work at all.

If you still aren't sure if a career in emergency response is right for you, try a self-assessment questionnaire or a career aptitude test. There are many good ones on the web. As an example, the career resource website Monster.com includes its favorite free self-assessment tools at www.monster.com/career-advice/article/best-free-career-assessment-tools. The *Princeton Review* also has a very good aptitude test geared toward high schoolers at www.princetonreview.com/quiz/career-quiz.

This chapter could just as well have been titled "How to Not End Up Miserable at Work." Because really, what all this is about is achieving happiness. After all, unless you're independently wealthy, you're going to have to work. That's just a given. If you work for eight hours a day starting at age eighteen and retiring at age sixty-five, you're going to spend around one hundred thousand hours at work. That's about eleven years! Your life will be much, *much* better if you find a way to spend that time doing something you enjoy, that your personality is well suited for, and that you have the skills to become good at. Plenty of people don't get to do this, and you can often see it in their faces as you go about your day interacting with people who are working. In all likelihood, they did not plan their careers very well and just fell into a random series of jobs that were available.

> The whole point of career planning is not to overwhelm you with a seemingly huge endeavor, it's to maximize happiness. Your ultimate goal should be to match your personal interests and goals with your preparation plan for college and career. Practice articulating your plans and goals to others. When you feel comfortable doing this, that means you have a good grasp of your goals and your plan to reach them.

Planning the Plan

You are on a fact-finding mission of sorts. A career fact-finding plan, no matter what the field, should include these main steps:

- Take some time to consider and jot down your interests and personality traits. Are you a people person, or do you get energy from being alone? Are you creative or analytical? Are you outgoing or shy? Are you organized or creative—or a little of both? Take a career counseling questionnaire (found online or in your guidance counselor's office) to find out more. Consider whether your personal likes and preferences meld well with the careers you are considering.
- Think about how you've done at school and how things have worked out at any temporary or part-time jobs you've had so far. In your opinion, what are you really good at? What have other people told you you're good at? What are you not very good at right now, but would like to become better at? What are you not very good at, and you're okay with not getting better at?
- Now forget about work for a minute. In fact, forget about needing to ever have a job again. You've won the lottery—congratulations! Now answer these questions: What are your favorite three ways to spend your

time? For each of those things, can you describe why you think you are particularly attracted to it? If you could get up tomorrow and do anything you wanted all day long, what would it be?

Take out your list of traits and look it over. Pretend you're not you. Instead, you're the hiring manager at a company. What kind of job might be good for the person who wrote what you're reading? Does he or she sound like someone who would work well with others? Do you think this person would work better on his or her own or as part of a team? (For example, if you wrote down a sport as a favorite thing to do, was it something like tennis, swimming, or wrestling? If so, it may be that you prefer to achieve things more on your own, on your own terms. If you wrote down football, basketball, softball, or volleyball, it could be that you're more comfortable working together with others to achieve a common goal.)

Now it's time to do fact-finding about the career itself:

- Find out as much as you can about the day-to-day work of first responders. In what kinds of environments do they work? Who do they work with? How demanding is the job? What are the challenges? Chapter 1 of this book is designed to help you in this regard.
- Find out about educational requirements and schooling and certification expectations. Will you be able to meet any rigorous requirements? Chapter 3 will help you understand the educational paths and certification requirements.
- Seek out opportunities to volunteer or shadow those doing the job. Use your critical-thinking skills to ask questions and consider whether this is the right environment for you.
- Build a timetable for taking required certifications and exams such as the SAT and ACT, applying to schools, visiting schools, and making your decision. You should write down all important deadlines and have them at the ready when you need them.
- Continue to look for employment that matters during your college years—internships and work experiences that help you get hands-on experience and knowledge about your intended career.
- Find a mentor who is currently working in your field of interest. This person can be a great source of information, education, and connections.

Don't expect a job (at least not at first); just build a relationship with someone who wants to pass along his or her wisdom and experience. Coffee meetings or even e-mails are a great way to start.

> "Some [fire] departments have explorer programs, which are a great opportunity for young people. Visit firehouses and look at going to school for a fire science degree. It's getting more and more important to have a degree. Get good grades."—Matt Hahn, twenty-year veteran firefighter

Where to Go for Help

If you're aren't sure where to start, your local library, school library, and guidance counselor's office are great places to begin. Search your local or school library for resources about finding a career path and finding the right schooling that fits your needs and budget. Make an appointment with or e-mail a counselor

A mentor can help you in many ways.

to ask about taking career interest questionnaires. With a little prodding, you'll be directed to lots of good information online and elsewhere. You can start your research with these sites:

- The Bureau of Labor Statistics' (BLS) Career Outlook site at www.bls.gov/careeroutlook/home.htm. The US Department of Labor's Bureau of Labor Statistics site doesn't just track job statistics, as you learned in chapter 1. An entire section of the BLS website is dedicated to helping young adults looking to uncover their interests and to match those interests with jobs currently in the market. Check out the section called "Career Planning for High Schoolers." Information is updated based on career trends and jobs in demand, so you'll get practical information as well.
- The Mapping Your Future site at www.mappingyourfuture.org. This site helps you determine a career path and then helps you map out a plan to reach those goals. It includes tips on preparing for college, paying for college, job hunting, résumé writing, and more.
- The Education Planner site at www.educationplanner.org. With separate sections for students, parents, and counselors, this site breaks down the task of planning your career goals into simple, easy-to-understand steps. You can find personality assessments, get tips on preparing for school, read Q&As from counselors, download and use a planner worksheet, read about how to finance your education, and more.
- The TeenLife site at www.teenlife.com. Calling itself "the leading source for college preparation" this site includes lots of information about summer programs, gap year programs, community service, and more. Promoting the belief that spending time out "in the world" outside of the classroom can help students do better in school, find a better fit in terms of career, and even interview better with colleges, this site contains lots of links to volunteer and summer programs.

Use these sites as jumping-off points and don't be afraid to reach out to real people such for more assistance:

- Ask to talk to a high school guidance counselor about first responder careers. He or she will likely be able to offer you lots of information about local explorer programs, possible ride-along opportunities, camps, and other career opportunities.

- If you're still really confused and feel like you're no closer to knowing what you want to do, you may want to consult with a career coach or personal coach to help you refine your understanding of your goals and how to pursue them. These professionals specialize in figuring out what sorts of careers and jobs may be appropriate for different people.

- Interview people in your community who are working in any jobs that you are considering. Feel free to ask them anything—what they enjoy about their work, what they find the most challenging, how they entered the field, advice on getting started, whether they would be willing to help you or provide a recommendation, and so on. You may even be able to visit them at their workplace and see firsthand what's involved. How do you find these people? Start asking around. You can ask your parents, your parents' friends, your teachers, and your school's guidance counselors. You could also search online using your hometown and the job title as keywords.

WHAT IF I DROPPED OUT OF HIGH SCHOOL?

In many ads for jobs, you'll see something like, "High school diploma or equivalent required." What does *equivalent* mean? It means you passed the General Educational Development exam and earned a GED. Once you earn that credential, you can use it like a high school diploma to pursue further technical, vocational, or college education and to apply for jobs.

In most states you must be at least sixteen years old to sit for the GED exam, and in some states you must be eighteen. The exam covers four subject areas: math, language arts, science, and social studies. The GED exam is now administered only on computer, so you need to at least know how to work a mouse and keyboard. And you should be prepared to settle in, because completing the test usually takes all day.

You can register for the GED exam at www.ged.com. The website will also tell you everything you need to know about taking the exam, including when and where you can take it and any fees you'll need to pay.

Making High School Count

Regardless of the career you choose, there are some basic yet important things you can do while in high school to position yourself in the most advantageous way. Remember—it's not just about having the best application, it's also about figuring out which areas of emergency response you actually would enjoy and which ones don't suit you.

- Use the summers to get as much experience as you can. Explorer programs, internships, and ride-alongs are all options you can find if you do enough digging. Volunteer in as many settings as you can.
- Hone your communication skills in English, speech, and debate. You'll need excellent communication skills in a job where you'll have to speak with everyone from patients to criminals to fellow employees.
- Learn first aid and CPR. These important skills are useful regardless of your profession but are critical for first responders.

You will almost certainly need more training beyond your high school courses, but high school is the best place to learn the basics of many skills you will use in emergency response. The following are some high school courses that can be of great benefit to anyone seeking work in emergency response services:

- *Science/Biology/Chemistry:* Science is a method of understanding the world through evidence and reason. A thorough understanding of humans' biological and chemical systems is critical to any emergency services profession.
- *Math:* You want to take as much math as you can, and at the highest level you can reasonably attain. Math teaches patience, logic, and discipline, and it trains your analytical and problem-solving skills.
- *English/Language Arts/Communication:* The better you can communicate with others, the more efficient and effective you will be on the job. This is something employers truly value. And it's not just verbal skills that are important. Being able to communicate accurate complex medical information clearly—to patients and their family members as well as to fellow employees—is an important component of success in first responder careers.

- *Social Studies:* You may not see right away why studying history, government, or psychology would be necessary to make a traffic stop. But the fact is, to get along smoothly in the modern workplace you need to know some background on your own culture and its institutions. Employers want their employees to be well-rounded and knowledgeable, and to be able to carry on conversations with people from different backgrounds. For example, psychology provides insights into why people do what they do and what their behavior says about them—you can rest assured that this comes in handy when you're a police officer. History tells us why things are the way they are and where these things came from. All this knowledge makes you a more well-rounded individual who can interact with the public in meaningful and positive ways.

BUILDING A FUTURE FOR
MOBILE INTEGRATED HEALTHCARE

Michael Kaufmann.
Courtesy of Michael Kaufmann

Michael Kaufmann became certified as an EMT in 1992 while studying biology in college. Within six months of taking that initial EMT class, he was hooked on emergency medicine. He attended the Indiana University School of Medicine and was a flight physician during his residency. He then returned to Indianapolis to become an emergency physician, where he has worked for eighteen years. He has also served as the EMS medical director for a large local hospital and all of its EMS partners, which served several nearby communities. In 2013 he became one of the first physicians in the country to become board certified in EMSs, and in 2018 he became the Indiana State EMS medical director through the Indiana Department of Homeland Security.

Can you explain how you became interested in being an EMT?

While in college, I knew that I loved biology and the life sciences, but didn't know yet what I wanted to do with my career. I was interested in healthcare, but didn't really see myself as a doctor.

The local community hospital offered a basic EMT training program, and within six months of enrolling in that class, I was going down a completely different career path! I was hooked on emergency medicine. I worked as an EMT while in school and then went to medical school and became an emergency physician. The basic EMT class gives you an introduction to medical pathophysiology and healthcare in general. It was a great way to get a basic-level understanding of healthcare. It allows you to function as a healthcare provider at a basic level. You get your foot in the door and can see if you like it. Also, you can go a lot of different directions with it—EMT, paramedic, EMS, advanced practice paramedic, physician's assistant, nurse, nurse practitioner, and more.

That initial EMT training class really helped me fall in love with emergency medicine. If it weren't for that class, I might have become a biomedical researcher.

What is a typical day in an EMT's job?

EMTs respond to 911 calls on potentially the worst days of people's lives. Or they might provide assistance at a school due to an injury. They also do a lot of noncritical care, such as car seat safety inspections, or help people with social services issues. They might act as a social worker or a healthcare provider, depending on a person's needs. Being an EMT requires a lot of different skills to help someone in their time of need.

The EMT and paramedic job is performed under a set of written treatment protocols. You deliver care based on protocols and guidelines created by your physician medical director. All EMS provider organizations have a physician medical director who sets up protocols and reviews the care given. They are employed typically by the hospital or by the organization to oversee clinical care. The EMT does patient assessments, such as taking a history, performing exams, and rendering care or treatment based on their training and the protocols they follow.

What do you think is the best part of being an EMT?

Being able to help people. They are calling you in maybe a life-and-death situation, and you can help them. You need to use your clinical judgment and provide care, and it may be as impactful as saving a life! Also, with emergency care in general, you get to treat a wide variety of problems. The variety is a definite benefit as well.

What's the challenging part of this profession?

Life-and-death situations can be difficult, and there are people you see who you can't save. Mentally, that is very difficult to process. You witness people die and then you have to interact with their families. This deserves special attention—the degree of secondary trauma that emergency care providers deal with. It's difficult mentally and emotionally.

To cope with that trauma, you need to focus on the good as well. Bad outcomes are horrible, of course, but there are also lots of good outcomes. You may save someone's life because of the medicine you give them, or you might help deliver a baby in the ambulance. Use those positive experiences. Also, talking about your bad experiences and using peer support to talk through them is very important. We use post-incident debriefings and talk about cases that were very difficult or serious. Don't keep it bottled up inside.

What's the most surprising thing about your career choice?

What's surprising sometimes is how impactful your actions can be to the people you care for. You can lose sight of how that affects someone's life. Someone might contact you later and remind you of the care you gave them during an accident, for example. That can surprise you.

Where do you see the field going from here?

I am humbled and honored to have been selected as the state EMS medical director. We are at a pivotal point for EMTs and first responders—they outnumber other healthcare providers two to one. If we don't change the way that healthcare in general is delivered, healthcare will struggle, and hospitals and EMS organizations will close. Up until now, EMTs have responded reactively. They wait for someone to call who is sick or injured.

We need to adapt EMS care to be proactive—we need to be out there before someone breaks his leg, for example, doing fall assessments, checking on people who've just been released from the hospital to ensure they can get their prescriptions, or making sure they can get to their doctor visit. We need to fully embrace mobile integrated healthcare, also called community paramedicine.

The EMT profession needs to take a more proactive role, which means preventing people from needing to call 911—preventive healthcare, transportation to appointments, aging in place, chronic care management, and so on. Much like the original fire service evolved to become in large part about fire prevention, we want EMTs and paramedics to focus more on preventive healthcare so people can avoid the 911 calls.

EMS personnel need to become full-fledged healthcare providers, rather than just providers of transportation. If not, we will become extinct.

What is your advice to a young person considering this career?

The various levels of first responders help you get your feet wet—you can really get a feel as to what emergency care is all about. Don't get into it too early, because there's a low passing rate for high school students. You need the right foundation. Start with the emergency medical responder (EMR) course, then take the EMT course, then the paramedic course. That helps lay the foundation.

The wrong reason for getting into emergency services, for one, is doing it for the money. It's not a high-paying job, although we are creating new roles and responsibilities to help with that, such as EMTs who work at the hospital. Roles in mobile integrated healthcare are expanding the responsibilities of its EMT and paramedic workforce.

How can a young person prepare for this career while in high school?

Get involved in a class, but make sure you are ready to do it. You can volunteer at a hospital in emergency medicine, or you can become a scribe. You work in the ER alongside the emergency physician. Find a way to see patients firsthand and expose yourself to the field. If you get out there and volunteer in the field, doors will open up for you.

Educational Requirements

The educational and certification requirements for first responder careers differ across these varied fields and also differ depending on where you plan on serving. The nice thing is that, with a few exceptions, you can enter a first responder profession at any of a number of different levels and with very little postsecondary education. Firefighters and police officers can enter their respective academies directly from high school, with little or no experience, and can then be trained completely by their employer or by a third party.

For EMTs and paramedics, as long as you are certified in the state in which you want to practice, you don't always need a formal degree. The following sections cover the traditional requirements in detail and then cover a few exceptions as well.

EDUCATIONAL REQUIREMENTS FOR FIREFIGHTERS

Although beginning a career as a firefighter doesn't typically require any formal education beyond a high school diploma or a GED, having some secondary education classes, an associate's degree in fire science, or certification as an EMT or paramedic can give you an advantage when the hiring pool is large and competitive. This extra training shows your interest and dedication and can lead to additional opportunities. Many firefighters say that having some kind of education is becoming more and more important to getting your boot in the door.

You will be expected to pass written, physical, and medical examinations prior to being considered for a job opening. This is where some formal post-secondary education can really help. Being able to write well and take tests well can be the difference between you and the next potential recruit.

Once you are hired as a new recruit, you'll participate in stringent physical training exercises and classroom work at the academy before you can enter the field. New recruits attend fire academy, usually run by the fire department or by the state, for twelve to fourteen weeks. The academy includes classroom instruction covering fire science technology and practical training, whereby recruits learn how to fight fires with standard equipment, including axes, chainsaws, fire extinguishers, and ladders. After graduating from academy, most firefighters work on probationary status for one year, during which time they receive additional training and supervision to ensure they are honing and continuing to learn their skills.

In addition, most firefighters in the United States must be certified as EMTs before they are allowed in the field, although this depends on the city or municipality.[1] EMT training can take up to one year and results in EMT-Basic certification.

GETTING A CERTIFICATE OR DEGREE IN FIRE SCIENCE

Certificates, associate's degrees, and bachelor's degrees in fire science are available at vocational colleges and four-year universities. Many of these programs are run by fire academies, which are usually associated with both the school and the local fire department.

Students in a fire science program study various fire investigation methods as well as techniques for controlling a fire. These programs also typically include instruction in fire prevention and teaching fire safety to the public. Fire science students are also taught basic first aid, CPR, and proper handling of hazardous materials.[2]

In addition to the training and certification, you must be at least eighteen years of age, be a citizen of the United States, and have no felonies to work as a firefighter. Many departments and states require a minimum age of twenty-one. Be sure to look into your specific local and state qualifications before you commit to extra schooling.

EDUCATIONAL REQUIREMENTS FOR POLICE OFFICERS

If you want to be a police officer, you need at least a high school diploma or equivalent. In addition, many federal agencies and some local and state police departments require some college coursework or even a college degree. Many community colleges, four-year colleges, and universities have programs in law enforcement and criminal justice; a degree from one of these programs can give you an advantage during the recruitment process. Be sure to check with your local and state agencies for their specific qualifications.

Just as with the fire department, you will be expected to pass written, physical, and medical examinations prior to being considered for a job opening. This is where some formal postsecondary education can really help. Being able to write well and take tests well can be the difference between you and the next potential recruit.

"Having some college experience helps you in many ways as a police officer. As an example, we had 570 people take our entry-level civil service exam, and 111 people failed it. On the other hand, the certified officers who take that exam, who must have at the minimum two years of college to be in the academy, have a very, very low failure rate. College experience really helps with the promotional exams, too. These include scenario-based and written sections, with policy laws, local ordinances, etc. Having a formal education helps with all these tests. You do a lot of interviewing and writing, and college helps with this, too."—Maureen O'Brien, twenty-seven-year veteran police officer

Once you are hired as a new recruit, you must graduate from the agency's training academy program, which usually takes about five months to complete, before completing a period of on-the-job training, a process similar to that for firefighters. These programs and their qualifications are discussed in more depth in chapter 3.

In addition to the training and education mentioned here, you usually must be at least twenty-one years of age (in a few places you can be as young as

Firearms training is part of police training academy.

eighteen), be a citizen of the United States, and have no felonies. You must also meet stringent physical and personal qualifications.

EDUCATIONAL REQUIREMENTS FOR EMTS AND PARAMEDICS

As mentioned in chapter 1, there are essentially three levels of EMT training, the third and most advanced one being paramedic certification.

EMT-Basic

The entry-level EMT certification, called EMT-Basic, trains students in basic EMT skills. Most basic certification courses have two components: a skills course and a lab course. The basic skills course teaches students how to assess a patient's condition and provide basic care for common conditions. The basic lab portion of the course is where students practice these skills. At a minimum, you must accumulate about 110 hours of training during this certification process.[3]

EMT-Intermediate

The EMT-Intermediate certification is the next step in EMT certification. EMT-I certification courses train students in more complex procedures. In most states, you must obtain EMT-B certification before you can enroll in an EMT-I course, because the intermediate course builds on the skills learned in the basic course. The EMT-I certification involves about two hundred to four hundred hours of training, and you'll then be qualified to perform more advanced duties, such as inserting IVs, intubating patients, and, in some states, administering drugs.[4]

It is best to obtain your EMT certification in the state in which you want to practice or in a state with stricter regulations. This is because regulations and requirements vary from state to state. Some states require the National Registry of Emergency Medical Technicians (NREMT) exam to be passed for all three certification levels, while others require it only for paramedic certification.[5]

EMT-Paramedic

The EMT-Paramedic certification is the highest level. To begin an EMT-P certification course, you must have completed both your EMT-B and EMT-I certifications. Then you will complete about two additional years of training, which includes classwork, lab work, and fieldwork. EMT-P certification courses focus on the advanced practice of medicine, including pharmacology, cardiology, and anatomy. To receive EMT-P certification, you usually have to complete an internship working in a hospital or ambulance.[6]

Networking

There's an old saying: "It's not what you know, it's who you know." And actually, in many cases, it's really who *they* know. Networking is a way to cultivate a web of relationships and use those relationships to make new ones. The connections

Networking with others is a great way to make contacts and find mentors.

and affiliations between people and groups of people make up what's called a social network. Social networking is powerful and has become very important in the modern workplace. About 85 percent of job opportunities are found through personal contacts.

THE CONCEPT OF SOCIAL NETWORKING

Imagine you have ten contacts in your social network. You could represent yourself as a dot in the middle, and your contacts as ten dots arranged in a circle around you. Then you could draw a line connecting you to each of them, like spokes on a bike wheel. Now imagine that each of your contacts knows ten people. Draw ten dots in a circle around each of the original ten dots and lines connecting those dots to their new dots. And of course, each of those *new* dots would also have ten dots, and so on.

What happened here, and what does it mean? It means your original ten contacts could potentially introduce you to one hundred new contacts. And *those* contacts could then introduce you to one thousand new contacts. As you can see, this simple concept swiftly starts adding up to big numbers. In fact, you would only have to go through three more rounds of drawing dots and you would be looking at more than a million people. And this example is conservative. Ten is a pretty small number to start with. You probably know a lot more than ten people, and each of them surely does, too.

This should give you a sense of the tremendous power of networking and why it's a major force in the business world. You can use networking as part of your work, and you can use it to find work. For example, I found all the first responders interviewed for this book through my own social network.

LinkedIn (www.linkedin.com) is a professional networking website specifically designed as a tool for cultivating business contacts. You can sign up for a free account on the website, and once you're signed up, you can start adding your own connections—the more, the better. You can search the site for positions and job titles, and LinkedIn will show you job openings and potential contacts who are contacts of your own contacts. In this way you can grow your number of professional contacts very quickly.

HOW TO NETWORK

Let's go back to the beginning, to those first ten dots you imagined drawing. Who are they? You are likely a young person without a lot of experience or contacts in the career field you may be interested in. How can you possibly network your way into a job in that field from where you are now?

Well, take a minute to really consider all the people you know. To begin with, you can probably count some or all of the following among your contacts right now:

- Parents
- Extended family members (aunts and uncles, cousins, perhaps grandparents)
- Friends (plus their parents and older siblings)
- Social media friends (Instagram, Snapchat, Twitter, Facebook, and so on)
- Teachers
- School administrators
- Coaches, club leaders, and sponsors (band, student council, yearbook)

- Clergy (pastor, rabbi, imam, priest)
- Employers and former employers
- Coworkers and former coworkers
- Neighbors
- Fellow church or club members (people you know from church or local clubs like 4-H, Lion's Club, Elks and Moose lodges, or Knights of Columbus)

Suddenly, it seems that you actually know quite a few people. Now, imagine how many people *they* know.

Don't forget that your high school guidance counselor can be a great source of information and connections as well.

You probably have an address book of some kind. If not, you can pick one up at a drug store or supermarket. Start writing down your contacts' names, phone numbers, and e-mail addresses. In many cases, you may only have a name. That's okay for now—write those down, too. These single names can serve as placeholders until you get their phone numbers and e-mail addresses.

Once you have a good number of contacts written down, come up with a short statement that says what kind of help you're looking for—for example:

Hi, _____. I'm looking for contacts in the _____ field as I consider my career choices. I am wondering if you might know someone I could talk to about this, to expand my network as I look for training and job opportunities? If you know of anyone who might be of help and you feel comfortable passing along their contact info, I would truly appreciate it!

Save your statement in generic form and then paste it into e-mails, instant messages, or text messages and customize it as appropriate each time—*don't* forget to customize it. If you prefer speaking on the phone, prepare a similar brief appeal that you can deliver verbally. Be brief, but don't be shy. Most people are more than willing to help if they can. Try to contact five people per day. That's enough to start making progress on expanding your network, but it's not enough to be overwhelming or burdensome. In no time, your address book will be filling up. For example, by the end of the first week you will have contacted thirty-five people and may have collected that many—or more—new contacts.

Once you've made a new contact, use a similar script or speech with that person, being sure to mention your common acquaintance by name. See if he or she is available to meet to discuss the career, training, and job opportunities you're interested in. If your meeting goes well, don't hesitate to ask if he or she knows of someone else you may want to talk to.

BUILDING COMMUNITY RELATIONS FOR THE FUTURE

Maureen O'Brien.
Courtesy of Maureen O'Brien

Lt. Maureen O'Brien serves with the Community Engagement Unit for the Grand Rapids Police Department in Grand Rapids, Michigan. She has been a police officer for twenty-seven years for the city of Grand Rapids and has served many roles during her career, including working on patrol, vice, and internal affairs, as well as mentoring youth through the Youth Police Explorer program since its inception in 2015.

Can you explain how you became interested in being a police officer?

In high school, my parents took my sister and me to Washington, DC. We toured the FBI headquarters, which piqued my interest in law enforcement. I was a competitive kid and enjoyed being active. I didn't think I'd ever want to sit behind a desk. As I went to community college, I educated myself and looked into policing. I wanted to go to the federal level, but at that time, you needed to speak another language or have other aptitudes that I didn't have, so I opted to go into local law enforcement. It was that FBI tour that really opened my eyes to law enforcement as a career.

Back then, it was very difficult to get a police job. About two thousand people took the test when I did—and twenty-three total were hired.

What are your main job duties?

I am currently the lieutenant of the Community Engagement Unit, which involves hiring, recruiting, background investigations, the intern program, the public information officer, and the boys and girls club officers.

We recruit for police officers and youth programs (intern programs for college students; police explorer program for anyone aged fourteen through twenty-one; youth police academy, which is a weeklong academy for juniors and seniors in high school; the chief's advisory board, open to youth in grades eight through twelve; and the on-base program for kids ages nine through twelve).

Our unit participates in many recruiting events, such as building tours (Boy Scouts, school groups), visiting churches to talk to their immigrant population and explain what we do, and other outreach. The goal is to strengthen relationships. We reach out to all types of communities. We go to block parties, festivals, career fairs, etc. We participated in over three hundred events last year!

We engage with the community in nonenforcement situations to strengthen relationships and trust within the community. We are constantly striving to have positive contacts with the community.

Working with the youth in these programs is encouraging and rewarding! They have real enthusiasm for the job. The explorer program, especially, is rewarding because it's a year long. Those kids really learn a lot, and community engagement is engrained in them by the time they are old enough to be hired. Helping them develop their skills is very rewarding.

What is your formal educational background? Did your education prepare you for your job?

I went to a two-year college to obtain my associate's degree and then transferred to Michigan State University, where I got a bachelor's in criminal justice.

Having some college experience helps you in many ways as a police officer. As an example, we had 570 people take our entry-level civil service exam, and 111 people failed it. On the other hand, the certified officers who take that exam, who must have at the minimum two years of college to be in the academy, have a very, very low failure rate.

The college experience really helps with the promotional exams, too. These include scenario-based and written sections, with policy laws, local ordinances, etc. Having a formal education helps with all these tests, in my opinion.

You do a lot of interviewing and writing, and college helps with this, too. People who write well generally go into our investigative units. Schooling can help you with listening and understanding skills and working in groups—these are all good in policing as well. Exposure to different cultures and an open worldview is also helpful.

You learn to multitask in college, too, and you need that with the caseload on the force.

So my education did prepare me as much as possible. However, the police academy and on-the-street learning are very educational.

What's the best part of being a police officer?

One thing for sure is working with our younger employees—the young officers and interns. You want to leave a legacy behind and be sure they are successful after you leave. Assisting them in getting the skills they need is very rewarding.

Also, interacting with employees and with the community and being allowed to be out and in the community is great. I enjoy not being behind a desk and doing something new every day. I am constantly learning.

What is the most surprising thing about your job?

How many different hats I would end up wearing! You become proficient at many things. You might act as a type of social worker, psychologist, etc. It's different every day—all cases are different. This is challenging and keeps you sharp.

What are some things that are especially challenging? Anything especially challenging being a female on the force?

The hardest part is, while you're on the street or on vice, witnessing the suffering of the people, especially with children and other very vulnerable people in the community. It's difficult to see it. You feel frustrated and helpless to remove them from inhumane environments.

In terms of being a female officer, it is a male-dominated career. I was an athlete and competitive growing up, so I was used to all that. But women can be too hard on themselves at times—don't second-guess yourself and your capabilities. Work hard. I am a big advocate of hard work. If you're not doing the work, you're not going to achieve your goals.

The guys are feeling the same worries and insecurities; they just might not vocalize it.

There were great women who went before me who retired. That's a huge advantage in vice because I was a good communicator, as a lot of women are. In 2013 I was promoted and back on patrol. I'd be out to dinner with a colleague, and a person in the community might see and thank the male officer but ignore me. Your desire to serve must come from the heart, as you will not always be recognized for it, nor should you really expect it, if you want a long career.

My advice to potential female officers: It's how you carry yourself and how you talk to people that will serve you well.

What are some characteristics of a good police officer? What people really don't fit well in law enforcement?

You must have a passion for this job. This is a calling—not really just a job. You must have a servant's heart, or it won't work. If you love it, it won't feel like work.

The motivation must be to serve. Personal integrity—that must come from within.

Also, you need good interpersonal skills and the ability to listen. A full 98 percent of the job is communicating! That's with citizens, suspects, coworkers, and so on. It's essential.

What are some of the challenges facing law enforcement and the people in it?

For law enforcement in general, numbers of potential recruits are low nationally, and every police department is hiring. It's a challenging time in law enforcement for staffing.

The negative attention that law enforcement is getting from media—that all officers are racist and not caring—is really hurting recruiting. People tend to see only the bad and not the good that police departments do every day.

This is really affecting how many young people want to pursue law enforcement. Nationwide, this is a real problem. There are tragically low numbers in academies all over the country. Then finding qualified candidates out of the low numbers can be challenging.

How do you fix community-police relations? That is something we are trying to do here. It's not something you do for a year—it's forever. I am optimistic that, over the coming years, those community relationships will be strengthened—which in turn will help recruitment.

What advice do you have for young people considering a career in law enforcement?

The Golden Rule! It's important to treat everyone as you would want your mother or father to be treated. It becomes pretty easy if you live by that rule.

Develop a life outside of police work. Have friends outside of work. Maintain that balance. It opens you up and keeps you more balanced.

Have a passion for this job, but also work hard! I will take hard workers any day. You have to put in the hours. Have a passion for the people you serve.

Constantly learn—don't ever stop learning. Be open-minded so you'll be well versed in many areas. Get proficient in many different areas, especially if you want to move up in leadership. It helps you a lot as a leader to have a variety of experiences.

How can a young person prepare for this career while in high school?

My biggest advice is to educate yourself. Do internships; go on ride-alongs. Get an accurate picture of the job—it's not like the shows on TV. Speak with police officers.

Find a police explorer or volunteer program so you can be sure you are making the right decision. That way, you'll be knowledgeable about your decision sooner during the fact-finding process.

Be involved with community outreach and volunteer in the community. For one, this may give you a leg up during the hiring process.

Finally, make good decisions! We lose a lot of people through background checks. Assaultive behavior, domestic situations, and certain misdemeanors can all rule you out. Patterns of bad behavior will certainly rule you out.

Any last thoughts?

It's a great career. It's been a journey and I've been blessed! I encourage everyone who has an interest in this field and a genuine desire to help people to pursue it.

Follow these important but simple rules for the best results when networking:

- Do your homework about a potential contact, connection, school, or employer before you make contact. Be sure to have a general understanding of what they do and why. But don't be a know-it-all. Be open and ready to ask good questions.
- Be considerate of professionals' time and resources. Think about what they can get from you in return for mentoring or helping you.
- Speak and write using proper English. Proofread all your letters, e-mails, and even texts. Think about how you will be perceived at all times.
- Always stay positive.
- Show your passion for the subject matter.

Summary

In this chapter, you learned even more about what it's like to be a first responder and what path you might take to get where you want to go. This chapter discussed the certification requirements of these different areas of emergency response, from college degrees to certification. You also learned about getting experience in the field before you enter college or training programs as well as during the educational process. Are you starting to picture your career plan? If not, that's okay, as there's still time.

Chapter 3 goes into a lot more detail about pursing the best educational path. The chapter covers how to find the best value for your education and includes discussion about financial aid and scholarships. At the end of chapter 3, you should have a much clearer view of the educational landscape and how and where you fit in.

3

Pursuing the Education Path

*I*f you've decided that you want to further pursue a career as a first responder, it's time to start looking at the best way to make that happen. Should you pursue a bachelor's or associate's degree from a college or university? Should you take a certification course in fire science, emergency medical technician (EMT), or law enforcement? When it comes time to start looking at colleges or postsecondary schools, many high schoolers tend to freeze up at the enormity of the job ahead of them. This chapter will help break down this process for you so it won't seem so daunting.

Finding the right learning institution is important, and it's a big step toward achieving your career goals and dreams. The last chapter covered the various educational requirements of these professions, which means you should now be ready to find the right institution of learning. This process should also be about finding the right fit so that you can have the best possible experience during your post–high school years.

> "My advice is to work toward a fire science degree while you network and meet firefighters at the station."—Matt Hahn, twenty-year veteran firefighter

Attending postsecondary schooling isn't just about completing the program requirements, getting certified, or even getting an associate's degree. It's also about learning how to be an adult, managing your life and your responsibilities, being exposed to new experiences, growing as a person, and otherwise becoming someone who contributes to society.

U.S. News & World Report puts it best when it reports that the education that fits you best is one that:

- Offers a degree that matches your interests and needs
- Provides a style of instruction that matches the way you like to learn

Accredited community colleges can be great places of learning for a fraction of the cost.

- Provides a level of academic rigor to match your aptitude and preparation
- Offers a community that feels like home to you
- Value you for what you do well[1]

According to the National Center for Educational Statistics (NCES), which is part of the US Department of Education, six years after entering college for an undergraduate degree, only 59 percent of students have graduated.[2] Barely half of those students will graduate from college in their lifetime.[3]

To Precertify or Not? That Is the Question

If you've read chapters 1 and 2, you probably realized by now that there are many different ways to enter a career in emergency response. Like all things in life, there are advantages and disadvantages of these different paths. They may all end up with the same or similar level of education and certification, but the timing of that process can differ depending on several factors. Let's break those down in more detail.

FIREFIGHTER OPTIONS

You can apply to fire departments with only a high school degree, although you usually have to be twenty-one to be eligible (in some places it's eighteen). If you are certain you want to be a firefighter and you either have a connection in a department or are fortunate to be applying when the numbers are low, this can be a successful way to enter the field. In addition to starting your career as soon as you're eligible, the benefits are that the department will usually pay for your certifications, and you'll be working (and earning a paycheck) as you are being trained and certified.

However, to increase your odds considerably in being hired, and—perhaps more importantly—to ensure that you are picking the right profession, consider the following classes and certifications, which you'll have to pay for yourself:

- *Classes or a degree in fire science:* You can take classes in fire science through your local university, community college, or even online and earn a fire science certificate, an associate's or bachelor's degree, or even a master's degree. Check out www.firesciencedegree.com for more information about the process and qualifications.
- *EMT certification:* Remember that there are three levels of EMT certification, and the higher the level you have, the better your chances are of being hired. See the section entitled "EMT/Paramedic Options" for details about how to become certified.

If you have a specific area, state, or even department that you have set your sights on working with, the smartest thing to do first is to research the requirements specific to that area or department. If it's a specific kind of firefighting you want to do, search the internet for information about the typical firefighter entering that kind of firefighting (average age of entry, education level, and so on). If it's a specific department that you want to work in, contact that department directly to find out how its recruitment process works. Finally, because they differ throughout the United States, be sure to determine the exact requirements of the state in which you plan on working.

> "To be a firefighter, you don't need to have an advanced degree, but it does help to have an education. The interview process can be intense. I encourage those interested to get an education in any degree, as it sets you apart. Even though you don't 'need' a degree, it is a huge leg up if you have one."—Tim Griffin, fifteen-year veteran firefighter

Once you are hired as a new recruit, you'll participate in rigorous physical training exercises and classroom work at the academy before you can enter the field. Recall that nearly all firefighters in the United States must be certified as EMTs before being allowed in the field, although this depends on the city or municipality.[4]

LAW ENFORCEMENT OPTIONS

As with firefighting, you can apply to law enforcement departments with only a high school degree, although you usually have to be twenty-one to be eligible (in some places it's eighteen). If you are certain you want to be a police officer and you either have a connection in a department or are fortunate to be applying when the numbers are low, this can be a successful way to enter the field. In addition to starting your career as soon as you're eligible, the benefits are that the department will usually pay for your certifications and you'll be working (and earning a paycheck) as you are being trained and certified.

However, having some postsecondary education experience can benefit you in many tangible and intangible ways as a police officer. Just as with the fire department, you will be expected to pass written, physical, and medical examinations prior to being considered for a job opening. In addition, officers have to be able to write and communicate as a daily part of their jobs. They write up reports that are read by other officers, judges, and people who were not on the scene, and are expected to be able to communicate the incident fully to all parties. Being able to write and take tests well is an important part of being promoted within the department, and having at least some formal postsecondary education can help in this regard.

Remember that many federal agencies and some local and state police departments require some college coursework or even a college degree. Be sure to check with your local and state agencies for their specific qualifications.

According to the website Discover Policing, which is managed by the International Association of Chiefs of Police, "You cannot go wrong with more education. Most departments, regardless of their requirements, give higher pay to recruits with four-year degrees."[5]

Once you are hired as a new recruit, you must graduate from the agency's training academy before completing a period of on-the-job training. These academy programs usually take three to eight months to complete and include classroom coursework covering legal studies, interpersonal studies, writing, and stress management, among others. The physical training portion—or skills development—usually involves defensive tactics certification, driver training, firearms qualifications, and more. The academy prepares you for the police force you will be assigned to when you graduate.

Many community colleges, four-year colleges, and universities have programs in law enforcement and criminal justice. The website www.criminaljusticedegreeschools .com provides a good overview of the kinds of degrees and classes you might want to consider. You can also visit www.discoverpolicing.org for a great overview of policing in general.

PATROL WATCH COMMANDER EXTRAORDINAIRE

Mark Ostapowicz.
Courtesy of Mark Ostapowicz

Lt. Mark Ostapowicz is a watch commander for the Grand Rapids Police Department in Grand Rapids, Michigan. He has been a police officer for twenty-seven years for the city of Grand Rapids. He began his career right after college, and in the years since he has served as a patrol officer, an undercover narcotics officer, on the SWAT team, as a sergeant supervising a team of officers, and as a training sergeant. As a lieutenant, he is currently the night watch commander, where he supervises third-shift patrol. He has also commanded the detective unit and internal affairs. In addition, he's been the commander of the crisis negotiation team for the past twelve years and a Use of Force instructor for twenty-four years.

Can you explain how you became interested in being a police officer?

For me, it's a family business—my father retired as a police officer and my younger brother is also a police officer. In college, I originally thought about teaching, but as I went along that path, I became unsure and didn't think it was for me anymore. My father arranged for a ride-along with an officer in his department, and I was hooked. I graduated from Wabash College on a Sunday and started the following Monday at the police academy, which was a sixteen-week program. I started in July of 1992.

What hooked me was the excitement. All the different calls made it so exciting. Nothing is predictable and you have no control over your day—you didn't know what your day held for you when it started. I liked that it was different every time. You must also like to help people. You have to care about people and want to help them. People call you at their worst. It's crisis time and they want your help.

What is a typical day/night on the job?

Currently, as the patrol watch commander, I start off doing a lot of administrative stuff, such as handling payroll, planning staffing, and giving out nightly car assignments, along with duties associated with the negotiating team. The rest of the night involves helping officers on their calls. I usually am not directly dispatched, so I am there to supervise or assist the officers. If a major incident occurs, I am in charge of that incident. I run the patrol shift. Anything that happens on my shift—I am in charge of it.

The night shift is busier than the day, but there aren't as many reports. The younger officers traditionally work the night shift, which is a lot of fun—they have energy and want to learn, and I enjoy mentoring them.

What's the best part of your job?

I enjoyed all the different positions I have worked; they have all been different. I really enjoyed the vice unit—we investigated narcotics, alcohol, gambling, and prostitution. You see the seedy side of life. The SWAT team was exciting. The best of the best are typically on the SWAT team—big vests, biggest rifles, fancy equipment, etc.

The role I have probably enjoyed the most is being a patrol sergeant. You're in charge of a team of officers—usually six or seven officers. You work with them every day in the same part of town and you get to know them and help them in their careers—you get to help the young guys become better officers.

What's the most challenging part of your job?

As a watch commander, the most challenging issue at the moment is that we are very short staffed, so allocating resources is difficult. We must make sure they are safe and all the calls get answered.

As a regular officer, the hardest thing is anytime you have to deal with children. Any trauma with children, including mental trauma or physical injuries, can be really hard to process.

What's the most surprising thing about your job?

Having grown up with a police officer, I knew what to expect. However, when you're on a really bad homicide—after it's all said and done and you reflect on the call—you are often surprised how much evil there really can be in the world. Or when you run into people who have given up and have no hope in their lives. They don't want your help.

All cops become cynical—if one tells you that they aren't, then they are lying. Any type of first responder—firefighters, emergency medical services (EMS), etc.—it happens to us all. You don't see a lot of good in the world. You see people at the bottom. A good support system with your family and friends and having interests outside of police work are all very important. It helps at the end of your shift to decompress and get away.

Did your education prepare you for the job?

I think so. In college you learn how to write well, and you need to do that as an officer. You have to tell lots of stories on paper. How your reports read is important, as you are telling the story to others (other officers, judges, and so on) who weren't on the scene. It must be accurate, detailed, and cohesive. Being able to communicate well is important, and college helps with that.

You also need people skills and to know how to communicate with all kinds of different people—which is mostly on-the-job training. You also need to be able to multitask—observe, drive, take calls, look for suspects, note any odd situations, and so on—all at once.

What is your advice to a young person considering this career?

Find a program through your high school or local police department. There are summer explorer programs and yearlong programs. Get involved locally so you can see if it really is for you. If you're not involved early on, and you've invested time and money and then figure out it's not for you, you're kind of behind the eight ball at that point. Get as much knowledge as you can prior to jumping in.

At the Grand Rapids Police Department, we have several opportunities for youth, including youth police academy during summers for high school students, yearlong explorer programs, and a mini police academy. We also have a college intern program where interns take actual police reports and deal with the public on a daily basis.

How can a young person prepare for this career while in high school?

Pay attention in your English and communications classes and learn how to write a good paper. Take interpersonal classes, too, and work on that skill. Those skills are good for any career. Also, there's forensics. If you're good in science, look at that route.

It's a very rewarding job; you're not going to be rich, but it's very fulfilling and satisfying when you can actually help someone. You are going to work long hours, weekends, nights, and holidays.

It's fun when you're on patrol and you run across a group of kids and they smile and are excited to see an officer. You have time to stop and show them the car and so on. Anytime you can have a positive influence on a young person—that feels good. Whether they want to be cops or not. Positive interaction is always fun.

What's next? Where do you see yourself going from here?

I am toward the end of my career—we can retire at fifty. I'll be watch commander a few more years. It's a physical job, and older people really can't do it well. Most officers retire around fifty or fifty-five.

EMT/PARAMEDIC OPTIONS

If you want to be an EMT or paramedic, you must be trained before you ever ride in an ambulance as a medical professional. Getting an EMT certification is also a great entry into firefighting or emergency medicine. Many professionals begin their careers working as EMTs and/or paramedics as they work their way through college or medical school, for example, or gain pertinent experience as an EMT as they apply to fire departments and become old enough to be accepted into those recruitment programs. Having EMT certification can give you an advantage when applying to law enforcement departments as well.

In chapter 2, you learned about the three levels of EMT certification available, which are summed up briefly here:

- EMT-Basic which is about 110 hours of training, trains students in basic EMT skills. It includes a skills component and a lab component. The basic skills course teaches students how to assess a patient's condition and provide basic care for common conditions. The basic lab portion is where students practice these skills.
- EMT-Intermediate, which is about two hundred to four hundred hours of training, teaches students more complex procedures. In most states, you must obtain EMT-B certification first. With the EMT-I certification, you are qualified to perform more advanced duties, such as inserting IVs, intubating patients, and, in some states, administering drugs.
- The EMT-Paramedic certification is the highest level. You must first complete the EMT-B and EMT-I certifications. Then you complete about two additional years of training, which includes classwork, lab work, and fieldwork. EMT-P certification courses focus on the advanced practice of medicine, including pharmacology, cardiology, and anatomy.

To be nationally registered as an EMS professional, you should be prepared to take the NREMT exam within two years of completing your certification course. Some states require it to be passed for all three certification levels, while others require it only for paramedic certification. For information about this exam, including how and where to take it, as well as a certification exam booklet, visit www.nremt.org.

CONTINUING EDUCATION

At every level of certification, EMTs must attend and complete additional training courses to keep their knowledge up to date and learn new technologies and methods. Depending on the state in which an EMT is certified, licenses must be renewed every two to three years.[6]

License renewal isn't the only reason for continuing your EMT education. The best EMTs use continuing education as a means to further develop their skills so that they become better at their jobs.

Recall from chapter 2 that it's smart to get your EMT certification in the state in which you'd like to practice, or a state with stricter regulations, because regulations and requirements vary from state to state. So how do you know how far to go with your certification before you enter the workforce? The answer to that question will depend on what you ultimately want to do, how competitive the departments are where you're applying, and how much money you have squirreled away for your continuing education. The first step is to start with the EMT-B coursework and apply and look for job opportunities while you are working toward that certification. Your path will open up and you'll have more opportunities—and more decisions to make—as you gain experience.

For Those Pursuing a Higher Education Degree

If you're currently in high school and you are serious about attending college for an associate's or bachelor's degree before you begin your career as an EMT, police officer, or firefighter, start by finding four to five schools in a realistic location for you that offer the degree, certificate, or program you want to pursue. Not every school near you or that you have an initial interest in will probably offer the program you want, so narrow your choices accordingly. With that said, consider attending a public university in your resident state, if possible, which will save you lots of money. Private institutions don't typically discount resident student tuition costs.

Be sure you research the basic grade point average (GPA) and SAT or ACT requirements of each school as well.

For students applying to associate's degree programs or higher, most advisers recommend that students take both the ACT and the SAT tests during the spring of their junior year at the latest. (The ACT test is generally considered more heavily weighted in science, so take that into consideration.) You can retake these tests and use your highest score, so be sure to leave time for a retake early in your senior year if needed. You want your best score to be available to all the schools you're applying to by January of your senior year, which will also enable your score to be considered with any scholarship applications. Keep in mind that these are general timelines—be sure to check the exact deadlines and calendars of the schools to which you're applying!

Once you have found four to five schools that offer the degree or certificate you want to pursue, spend some time on their websites studying the requirements for admission. Most colleges and universities list the average stats for the last class accepted to the program. Important factors in your decision about what schools to apply to should include whether or not you meet the requirements, your chances of getting in (but shoot high!), tuition costs and availability of scholarships and grants, location, and the school's reputation and licensure/graduation rates.

WHAT'S THE DIFFERENCE BETWEEN VOCATIONAL SCHOOL AND COLLEGE?

Both vocational school and college provide postsecondary education, both award degrees, but there are some pretty big differences:

- Colleges and universities are designed for four-year bachelor's and graduate degree programs. Vocational schools are geared toward two-year associate's degrees and various certificates for study lasting less than two years.
- In college, students take a wide variety of courses, some of which are outside their area of study. In vocational school, students study one subject with

a narrow focus and an emphasis on practical training for a specific job. This is why it only takes two years instead of four.

- A large percentage of college students live on or very near campus. Most vocational students commute to class, and many hold down outside jobs.
- Colleges and universities cost significantly more to attend, often two or three times what vocational schools cost.
- At a vocational college, you won't see huge lecture halls filled with a couple hundred students taking notes on a lecture by a professor who doesn't know their names. Classes at vocational schools are usually small (twenty to thirty students) and often involve hands-on training in shops and labs.

The importance of these characteristics will depend on your grades and test scores, your financial resources, and other personal factors. You want to find a school that has a good reputation that matches your academic rigor and practical needs.

THE MOST PERSONAL OF PERSONAL STATEMENTS

The personal statement you include with your application to college is extremely important, especially if your GPA and SAT/ACT scores are on the border of what is typically accepted. Write something that is thoughtful and conveys your understanding of and passion for the profession you are interested in, as well as your desire to practice in this field. Why are you uniquely qualified? Why are you a good fit for the university or college? These essays should be highly personal (the "personal" in personal statement). Will the admissions professionals who read it—along with hundreds of others—come away with a snapshot of who you really are and what you are passionate about?

Look online for some examples of good personal statements, which will give you a feel for what works. Be sure to check your specific school for length guidelines, format requirements, and any other guidelines you are expected to follow.

And of course, be sure to proofread it several times and ask a professional (such as your school writing center or your local library services) to proofread it as well.

What's It Going to Cost You?

So, the bottom line: what will your education end up costing you? Of course, this depends on many factors, including the type and length of degree you pursue; whether the school is a private for-profit, private not-for-profit, or public institution; how much in scholarships or financial aid you're able to obtain; your family or personal income; and many other factors. The College Entrance Examination Board tracks and summarizes financial data from colleges and universities all over the United States. (You can find more information at www.collegeboard.org.)

Public two-year colleges usually offer the most education value for your dollar. According to the College Board, in 2018 the average tuition at public two-year colleges in the United States was $3,440.[7] But not all public colleges will offer the program you're looking for. For vocational schools, average tuition depends greatly on where you live; for example, in New Jersey the average vocational school tuition is $9,167, and in New Mexico it's $3,125.[8]

Costs go up every year. Generally speaking, there is about a 3 percent increase in tuition each year. In other words, if you are expecting to attend college two years after this data was collected, you need to add approximately 6 percent to these numbers. The good news is that financial aid and scholarships can offset tuition costs somewhat.

The actual, final price (or net price) that you'll pay for a specific college is the difference between the published price (tuition and fees) to attend that college, minus any grants, scholarships, and education tax benefits you receive. This difference can be significant. In 2015–2016, the average published price of in-state tuition and fees for public four-year colleges was about $9,410. But the average net price of in-state tuition and fees for public four-year colleges was only about $3,980.[9]

This chapter discusses finding the most affordable path to get the degree you want. Later in this chapter, you'll also learn how to prime the pumps and get as much money for college as you can.

WHAT IS A GAP YEAR?

Taking a year off between high school and college, often called a gap year, is normal, perfectly acceptable, and almost required in many countries around the world. It is becoming increasingly acceptable in the United States as well. Even Malia Obama, President Obama's daughter, did it. Because the cost of college has gone up dramatically, it literally pays for you to know going in what you want to study, and a gap year—well spent—can do lots to help you answer that question.

Some great ways to spend your gap year include joining organizations such as the Peace Corps or AmeriCorps, enrolling in a mountaineering program or other gap year–styled program, backpacking across Europe or other countries on the cheap (be safe and bring a friend), finding a volunteer organization that furthers a cause you believe in or that complements your career aspirations, joining a Road Scholar program (see www.roadscholar.org), teaching English in another country (more information is available at www.gooverseas.com/blog/best-countries-for-seniors-to-teach-english-abroad), or work and earn money for college!

Many students will find that they get much more out of college when they have a year to mature and to experience the real world. The American Gap Year Association reports from alumni surveys that students who take gap years show greater civic engagement, higher college graduation rates, and GPAs in college.[10]

See the association's website at www.gapyearassociation.org for lots of advice and resources if you're considering this potentially life-altering experience.

Financial Aid and Student Loans

Finding the money to attend college—whether a two- or four-year college program, an online program, or a vocational career college—can seem overwhelming. But you can do it if you have a plan before you actually start applying to college. If you get into your top choice, don't let the sticker price turn you away. Financial aid can come from many different sources, and it's available to cover all different kinds of costs you'll encounter while getting your education, including tuition, fees, books, housing, and food.

The good news is that colleges and universities more often offer incentive or tuition discount aid to encourage students to attend. The market is often

Paying for your education can take a creative mix of grants, scholarships, and loans, but you can find your way with some help.

more competitive in the favor of the student, and colleges and universities are responding by offering more generous aid packages to a wider range of students than they used to. Here are some basic tips and pointers about the financial aid process:

- Apply for financial aid during your senior year. You must fill out the Free Application for Federal Student Aid (FAFSA) form, which can be filed starting October 1 of your senior year until June of the year you graduate.[11] Because the amount of available aid is limited, it's best to apply as soon as you possibly can. See https://studentaid.ed.gov/sa/fafsa to get started.
- Wait until you receive all offers from your top schools and then use this information to negotiate with your top choice to see if it will match or beat the best aid package you received.
- To be eligible to keep and maintain your financial aid package, you must meet certain grade/GPA requirements. Be sure you are very clear about these academic expectations and keep up with them.
- You must reapply for federal aid every year.

Watch out for scholarship scams! You should never be asked to pay to submit the FAFSA form ("free" is in its name) or be required to pay a lot to find appropriate aid and scholarships. These are free services. If an organization promises you that you'll get aid or that you have to "act now or miss out," these are both warning signs of a less-than-reputable organization.

You should also be careful with your personal information to avoid identity theft as well. Simple things like closing and exiting your browser after visiting sites where you entered personal information goes a long way. Don't share your student aid ID number with anyone, either.

It's important to understand the different forms of financial aid that are available to you. That way, you'll know how to apply for different kinds and get the best financial aid package that fits your needs and strengths. The two main categories that financial aid falls under are gift aid, which doesn't have to be repaid, and self-help aid, which includes loans that must be repaid and work-study funds that are earned. The next sections cover the various types of financial aid that fit into these areas.

GRANTS

Grants typically are awarded to students who have financial need, but can also be used in the areas of athletics, academics, demographics, veteran support, and special talents. They do not have to be paid back. Grants can come from federal agencies, state agencies, specific universities, and private organizations. Most federal and state grants are based on financial need.

Examples of grants are the Pell Grant, SMART Grant, and the Federal Supplemental Educational Opportunity Grant. Visit the US Department of Education's Federal Student Aid site at https://studentaid.ed.gov/types/grants-scholarships for lots of current information about grants.

SCHOLARSHIPS

Scholarships are merit-based aid that does not have to be paid back. They are typically awarded based on academic excellence or some other special talent, such as music or art. Scholarships can also be athletic-based, minority-based, aid for women, and so forth. These are typically not awarded by federal or state governments, but instead come from the specific school you applied to as well as private and nonprofit organizations.

Be sure to reach out directly to the financial aid officers of the schools you want to attend. These people are great contacts who can lead you to many more sources of scholarships and financial aid. Visit GoCollege's Financial Aid Finder at www.gocollege.com/financial-aid/scholarships/types for lots more information about how scholarships in general work.

LOANS

Many types of loans are available especially for students to pay for their post-secondary education. However, the important thing to remember here is that loans must be paid back, with interest. (This is the extra cost of borrowing the money and is usually a percentage of the amount you borrow.) Be sure you understand the interest rate you will be charged. Is this fixed or will it change over time? Are payments on the loan and interest deferred until you graduate (meaning you don't have to begin paying it off until after you graduate)? Is the loan subsidized (meaning the federal government pays the interest until you graduate)? These are all points you need to be clear about before you sign on the dotted line.

There are many types of loans offered to students, including need-based loans, non-need-based loans, state loans, and private loans. Two very reputable federal loans are the Perkins Loan and the Direct Stafford Loan. For more information about student loans, visit https://bigfuture.collegeboard.org/pay -for-college/loans/types-of-college-loans.

FEDERAL WORK-STUDY

The US federal work-study program provides part-time jobs for undergraduate and graduate students with financial need so they can earn money to pay for educational expenses. The focus of such work is on community service work and work related to a student's course of study. Not all schools participate in this program, so be sure to check with the school financial aid office at any schools you are considering if this is something you are counting on. The sooner you apply, the more likely you will get the job you desire and be able to benefit from the program, as funds are limited. See https://studentaid.ed.gov/sa/types/work-study for more information about this opportunity.

BEING A FIREFIGHTER IS BEING PART OF A FAMILY

Tim Griffin.
Courtesy of Tim Griffin

Tim Griffin is a firefighter and EMT at the fire department in Carmel, Indiana, a city outside of Indianapolis with about ninety thousand residents. He also serves as a public information officer and as a peer fitness instructor, which involves putting new recruits through their morning training regimen and keeping firefighters in shape. He has been with the Carmel Fire Department for fifteen years.

Can you explain the role of the public information officer as a part of fire services?

I am one of two public information officers in the department, and we run all of our social media, including the Twitter, Facebook, and website accounts. We disseminate stories about good things the fire department is doing, provide informational and educational fire safety information, and disseminate information about emergency situations to the media. We are on the scene at those emergencies and provide real-time information to the media for the benefit of the public. It's more marketing in nature. Taxpayers pay our salaries, so they should know what we do. Prevention is a big part of fire service, as well as hazardous materials, inspections, code enforcement, and, of course, emergency response.

What are your main job duties as a firefighter?

I am still on a fire truck, too. These are twenty-four-hour shifts, which is usually 7:00 a.m. to 7:00 a.m. We work the Kelly System, which is a schedule where you are "on" Wed., Fri., Sun., then off for four days. Then it rotates, so you would work Fri., Sun., Tues., and then be off four days.

You arrive in the morning of your twenty-four-hour shift, check out your personal equipment and the truck equipment, and replenish anything that needs it. Then we do house duties, which includes cleaning the house, having breakfast, and so on. Then we have EMS and fire training, perform inspections, give tours, and exercise.

Any time during that routine, if the tones go off, we drop everything and make emergency runs. We are the busiest truck in our county, and we make about eight to twelve runs a day on average. About 80 percent of that is EMS related; 20 percent is fire related.

Every day is different—you never really know what you are going to do. We might have seventeen runs, two fires, an inspection, and a tour all in one day! I like that—the best part is it's unique and you don't know what your day will hold.

The mobile integrated healthcare part of our efforts involves visiting homes of elderly or sick [people] who might have many calls out to their homes. It's preventive in nature to help these people avoid needing emergency care.

All the fire service personnel in our department are EMTs, and some are paramedics (close to an RN degree); we work under a blanket of a director. Most firefighters are also EMTs nowadays.

What is your formal educational background?

I was an education major originally. My senior year in high school, my best friends were involved in a head-on collision. I was following them and experienced the whole thing. Only the driver was buckled in. The guys in my car all ran up to the scene to assist in any way we could. We were lifeguards, so we had some basic training and were checking airways. The fire department showed up and used their extrication tools to get them out of the mangled vehicle and provide emergency services. Three of them were airlifted to the hospital. They all made full recoveries. That was a life-changing experience.

This experience stayed with me as I started college. While midway through college, I started taking fire science and then applying to fire departments. I originally attended Indiana University/Purdue University at Indianapolis and then took fire science at Ivy Tech, but I was hired on before I finished my degree.

What's the typical path to becoming a firefighter?

To be a firefighter in Indiana, you don't need a college degree. You have to be twenty-one, have a high school diploma or GED, be a citizen, and have no felonies. But it does help to have an education. The interview process can be intense. I encourage those interested to get an education in any degree, as it sets you apart. Even though you don't need a degree, it is a huge leg up if you have one.

Once you are hired, you go through a recruit class. It's a Monday-through-Friday class that includes working out, in-classroom training, being out on the fire ground, and EMT school. Once you finish the recruit class, you'll be out on shift. For a year, you are a probationary firefighter and receive extra training during that time. We want to make sure that our new firefighters are staying up on the skills they learned and are getting better.

A lot of what you learn is on-the-job experience. You also learn so much from other firefighters who are experienced. Talk with older firefighters at the firehouse is invaluable.

What's the best part of being a firefighter?

There are so many good parts! Getting to help people is probably the best. Most of us have a story like I have—about helping people. People do it to help others.

It's truly a brother- and sisterhood. We live together and eat together and live through life-threatening situations. You really become attached and become a family. Our families become families with the firefighters. The firefighter bond transcends location and department as well. I can go anywhere in this country with a firefighter shirt on and I'll have a great conversation with a fellow firefighter. It's really special.

Of course, there are good benefits, including a good pension and insurance. The time off is nice, but there is also time away. The oldest you can be in our department is seventy-one, but most retire in their late fifties to early sixties. That's why a good pension is so important.

What are some things you don't like about your job?

Being away from your family for twenty-four hours at a time is hard, especially when you have a family and young kids. You'll spend holidays at the station usually, unless you have high seniority.

The other thing that's really hard is when someone is injured or killed—especially a child.

What's the most surprising things about being a firefighter?

The bond with other firefighters is wonderful. I'm in it fifteen years, and I still enjoy the career. It has not become mundane.

What would be your dream job within this field?

I am doing it now! I'm still on a truck and helping people, but I also get to advertise what we do as the public information officer. Being the face of our department is really fun for me.

What are some characteristics of good firefighters? What kinds of people really don't fit well in this profession?

You need to work well on a team. You do everything in a team setting. It takes all moving parts working together.

You need a willingness to never stop learning! It's really changed in the fifteen years since I've been here. Yes, it's still "put the wet stuff on the red stuff," but the techniques, equipment, dangers, etc., have all changed significantly.

You need to have a servant's heart—you are a public servant. People call us on their worst day. Be compassionate and understanding. We are not judgmental and nondiscriminatory.

What are some of the challenges facing the industry and the people in it?

The health risks are significant—exposures that cause cancer, including lung, colon, testicular, and others. Firefighters are diagnosed with cancer at a much higher rate than the general public. The masks aren't doing it alone, because it's not just about what you're breathing in. The soot and plastics—in the form of carcinogens—are absorbing into our skin. The number of deaths yearly due to fires hasn't changed, even with better equipment. One simple way to deal with this is to clean the gear and get the carcinogens off. There are deep traditions about dirty gear signifying a seasoned firefighter, but that soot is killing our firefighters. Clean gear means healthy gear.

Mental health issues related to trauma is also a challenge. This is true with all first responders—we all see tragedy and trauma. The big change with fire services in recent years is to encourage firefighters to talk about their trauma and get help dealing with it. They aren't encouraged to be tough and deal with it on their own anymore.

What is your advice for a young person considering this career?

Do it—it's wonderful! Talk to lots of firefighters and research the career. Find out what it's like and how to get hired. Be a sponge and sit back and listen and learn. There are explorer programs, for example, and you can even simply interact with stations via social media.

How can a young person prepare for this career while in high school?

Some places have cadet fire programs or career paths to leave the high school and learn about fire service, first aid, CPR, and so on. Get involved in your community and volunteer. Whether it's athletics or a chess team or whatever, get on a team and learn to work well with others!

The military path or through ROTC is also a good entry into fire service. Postmilitary often become firefighters. You've learned to work with others, and you know how to deal with stressful situations.

We do a lot of community outreach, too. Get involved in these programs.

Can you talk about the EMS/EMT portion of your job?

That is our bread and butter—EMS calls happen every day. There are four EMTs on our engines and two EMTs on our ambulances. If you call 911, you get an engine and an ambulance. They both get sent. There are lots of moving parts, just like with a fire. We need to take histories, take vital signs, talk to the family, push the right meds, move the victim, maybe do CPR, and more. It was EMS that attracted me first, in terms of my friends' car collision.

I have also been a recipient of great EMT care. Two years ago I was sick with what seemed like a normal flu. I had lost a lot of fluids very fast. My wife drove me to our fire station, a mile away. I walked in and they immediately put me in an ambulance. My heart was racing (280 beats per minute) and my blood pressure was 60/40! I was in bad shape. They had to stop my heart twice. It turns out I was dehydrated and my stomach was distended and was pressing against my heart. I spent three days in the cardiac critical care unit. It was a bit of an ego blow, but as a recipient of getting the care I was used to giving, it has given me special empathy and insight into the experience. I'm even more grateful for and appreciative to this profession.

Making High School Count

If you are still in high school or middle school, there are still many things you can do now to help the postsecondary educational process go more smoothly. Consider these tips for your remaining years:

- Work on listening well and speaking and communicating clearly. Work on writing clearly and effectively.
- Learn how to learn. This means keeping an open mind, asking questions, asking for help when you need it, taking good notes, and doing your homework.
- Plan a daily homework schedule and keep up with it. Have a consistent, quiet place to study.
- Talk about your career interests with friends, family, and counselors. They may have connections to people in your community who you can shadow or who will mentor you.
- Try new interests and activities, especially during your first two years of high school.
- Be involved in extracurricular activities that truly interest you and say something about who you are and who you want to be.

Kids are under so much pressure these days to do it all, but you should think about working smarter rather than harder. If you are involved in things you enjoy, your educational load won't seem like such a burden. Be sure to take time for self-care, such as sleep, unscheduled downtime, and activities that you find fun and energizing. See chapter 4 for more ways to relieve and avoid stress.

Summary

This chapter looked at all the aspects of postsecondary schooling that you'll want to consider as you move forward. Remember that finding the right fit is especially important, as it increases the chances that you'll stay in school and finish your degree or program—and have an amazing experience while you're there. The careers under the first responders umbrella have varying educational requirements, which means that finding the right educational fit can be very different depending on your career aspirations.

In this chapter, you learned about how to get the best education for the best deal. You also learned a little about scholarships and financial aid, how the SAT and ACT tests work, and how to write a unique personal statement that eloquently expresses your passions.

Use this chapter as a jumping-off point to dig deeper into your particular area of interest, but don't forget these important points:

- Take the SAT and ACT tests early in your junior year so you have time to take them again if you need to. Most schools automatically accept the highest scores.
- Make sure that the school you plan to attend has an accredited program in your field of study. Some professions follow national accreditation policies, while others are state mandated and therefore differ across state lines. Do your research and understand the differences.
- Don't underestimate how important school visits are, especially in the pursuit of finding the right academic fit. Come prepared to ask questions not addressed on the school's website or in the literature.
- Your personal statement is a very important piece of your application that can set you apart from other applicants. Take the time and energy needed to make it unique and compelling.

- Don't assume you can't afford a school based on the sticker price. Many schools offer great scholarships and aid to qualified students. It doesn't hurt to apply. This advice especially applies to minorities, veterans, and students with disabilities.
- Don't lose sight of the fact that it's important to pursue a career that you enjoy, are good at, and are passionate about! You'll be a happier person if you do so.

At this point, your career goals and aspirations should be jelling. At the very least, you should have a plan for finding out more information. And don't forget about networking, which was covered in more detail in chapter 2. Remember to do the research about the school or degree program before you reach out and especially before you visit. Faculty and staff find students who ask challenging questions much more impressive than those who ask questions that can be answered by spending ten minutes on the school's website.

Chapter 4, goes into detail about the next steps—writing a résumé and cover letter, interviewing well, follow-up communications, and more. This information is not just for college grads; you can use it to secure internships, volunteer positions, summer jobs, and other opportunities. In fact, the sooner you can hone these communication skills, the better off you'll be in the professional world.

4

Writing Your Résumé and Interviewing

No matter which path you decide to take—whether you enter the workforce immediately after high school, go to college first and then find yourself looking for a job, or maybe do something in between—having a well-written résumé and impeccable interviewing skills will help you reach your ultimate goals. This chapter provides some helpful tips and advice to build the best résumé and cover letter, how to interview well with all your prospective employers, and how to communicate effectively and professionally at all times.

The advice in this chapter isn't just for people entering the workforce full-time, either; it can help you score an internship, explorer program, or summer job, or help you give a great interview to impress the admissions office or local firehouse or police station. The principles discussed here remain important throughout your working life, on and off the job. Learn them now, cultivate them as automatic habits, and they will serve you for as long as you're in the working world.

The chapter also has some tips for dealing successfully with stress, which is an inevitable by-product of a busy life.

Creating a Résumé

If you're a teen writing a résumé for your first job, you likely don't have a lot of work experience under your belt yet. Because of this limited work experience, you need to include classes and coursework that are related to the job you're seeking, as well as any school activities and volunteer experience you have. While you are writing your résumé, you might discover some talents and recall some activities you did that you forgot about but that are still important to add.

Think about volunteer work, side jobs you've held (babysitting, volunteering at the firehouse, dog walking, etc.), and the like. A good approach at this point in your career is to build a functional résumé, which focuses on your abilities rather than work experience, and it's discussed in detail next.

PARTS OF A RÉSUMÉ

The functional résumé is the best approach when you don't have a lot of pertinent work experience, as it is written to highlight your abilities rather than your experience. (The other, perhaps more common, type of résumé is called the chronological résumé, which lists a person's accomplishments in chronological order, most recent jobs listed first.) This section breaks down and discusses the functional résumé in greater detail.

Here are the essential parts of your résumé, listed from the top down:

- *Heading:* This should include your name, address, and contact information, including phone, e-mail, and website if you have one. This information is typically centered at the very top the page.
- *Objective:* This is a one-sentence statement that tells the employer what kind of position you are seeking. This should be modified to be specific to each potential employer.
- *Education:* Always list your most recent school or program first. Include date of completion (or expected date of graduation), degree or certificate earned, and the institution's name and address. Include workshops, seminars, explorer programs, and related classes here as well.
- *Skills:* Skills include computer literacy, leadership skills, organizational skills, and time-management skills. This is where you can list certifications or licenses. Be specific in this area, when possible.
- *Activities:* Activities can be related to skills. Perhaps an activity listed here helped you develop a skill listed above. This section can be combined with the Skills section, but it's often helpful to break these apart if you have enough substantive things to say in both areas. Examples include sports teams, leadership roles, community service work, clubs and organizations, and so on.
- *Experience:* Here you should include the jobs you have worked in, in reverse chronological order. The first one on your list may well be your

current or recent apprenticeship. Don't worry if some of the jobs you've had don't seem particularly relevant to what you're applying for. Include them anyway and do your best to make them seem relevant. You're young, and it's understood that you haven't had a lot of time to gain direct experience in the field you're after. Of course, you should emphasize any jobs that *are* especially relevant. This is where you can include part-time jobs, summer jobs, and volunteer experience.

- *Interests:* This section is optional, but it's a chance to include special talents and interests. Keep it short, factual, and specific. Show your passion for the field here.

- *References:* It's best to say that references are available on request. If you do list actual contacts, list no more than three and make sure you inform your contacts that they might be contacted.

The first three parts above are pretty much standard, but the others can be creatively combined or developed to maximize your abilities and experience. These are not set-in-stone sections that every résumé must have. As an example, consider the mock functional résumé in figure 4.1, which uses a combination of these sections to accentuate Ryan's strengths.

If you're still not seeing the big picture here, it's helpful to look at student and part-time résumé examples online to see how others have approached this process. Search for "functional résumé examples" to get a look at some examples.

RÉSUMÉ-WRITING TIPS

Regardless of your situation and why you're writing the résumé, there are some basic tips and techniques you should use:

- Keep it short and simple. This includes using a simple, standard font and format. Using one of the résumé templates included in your word processor software can be a great way to start.
- Use simple language. Keep it to one page.
- Highlight your academic achievements, such as a high GPA (above 3.5) or academic awards. If you have taken classes related to the job you're interviewing for, list those briefly as well.

Ryan Christopher

974 Audubon Circle
Portland, OR, 97035
Phone: 503-503-5030 E-Mail: rec2020@student.com

Objective

Seeking an entry-level position as a firefighter—eager to save life and property

Education

High School Diploma, June 2016
Westhaven High School, Portland, OR

6 credits in Fire Science at IUMA.edu

Areas of Expertise

- Hazard Identification
- Victim Stabilization
- CPR

- Immediate Rescue
- Hazmat Training
- Hands-on Experience Performing Fire-Suppression Duties

Key Achievements & Awards

Outstanding Community Service Award, 2018

Professional Experience

August 2016-September 2018, Two years experience working with Aurora Volunteer Fire Department, 2016-2018
June 2016-June 2017, Part-time volunteer, EMT Incorporated, Portland, OR

References

Available upon request

Figure 4.1. A functional-style résumé is a good template to use when you don't have a lot of work experience.

- Emphasize your extracurricular activities, internships, and the like. These could include clubs, sports, dog walking, babysitting, or volunteer work. Use these activities to show your skills and abilities.
- Use action verbs, such as *led, created, taught, ran,* and *developed.*
- Be specific and give examples.
- Always be honest.
- Include leadership roles and experience.
- Edit and proofread at least twice, and have someone else do the same. Ask a professional (such as your school writing center or your local library services) to proofread it for you also. Don't forget to run spell check.
- Unless specifically instructed not to, include a cover letter (discussed in the next section).

According to research by the job search site the Ladders (www.theladders.com), a recruiter spends an average of just six seconds reading each résumé.[1]

Your final product should be simple and clear. Don't get caught up in choosing fancy typefaces, elaborate graphics or color schemes, or funky staggered paragraphs or other design elements. Think about what the people who will be reading your résumé want. They want to, above all, save time. They don't want to be looking through résumés. It's not a fun job. It gets old very quickly. It tends to cause headaches. Make their job as easy as possible when they get to yours—they'll appreciate it.

Here are some final practical things to keep in mind when creating your résumé:

- Save it in a few different formats so it is ready to go at any time. Most of the time you'll be uploading the résumé online to companies, and the most commonly requested file formats are Microsoft Word, PDF, and plain text.
- Have several dozen all printed out and ready to give out at a moment's notice.
- Create customized versions for employers you're really interested in. If you're sending out twenty résumés, but five of them are going to places

where you'd be especially excited to work, create a special résumé for each one of those five. Carefully study what kind of company or organization each one is and what skills and experience they say they are looking for, and make your résumé to them reflect your best effort at being what they want.

- Highlight your accomplishments, not just the routine, day-to-day things you did in some past job. If there is anything in your experience you did that makes you stand out from the crowd, make it prominent.

THE COVER LETTER

Every résumé you send out usually includes a cover letter. This can be the most important part of your job search because it's often the first thing that potential employers read. By including the cover letter, you're showing the employers that you took the time to learn about their organization and address them personally. This goes a long way to show that you're interested in the position. See the sidebar called "Résumés, Cover Letters, and Online Job Applications," for exceptions to the standard cover letter approach.

Be sure to call the company or verify on the website the name and title of the person to whom you should address the letter or e-mail. This letter or e-mail should be brief. Introduce yourself and begin with a statement that will grab the person's attention. Keep in mind that employers potentially receive hundreds of résumés and cover letters or e-mails for every open position. You want yours to stand out. Important information to supply includes:

- Your name, address, phone number, and e-mail address
- The current date
- The recipient's name, title, company name, and company address
- Salutation

Then you begin the letter portion of the cover letter or e-mail, which should mention how you heard about the position, something extra about you that will interest the potential employer, practical skills you can bring to the position, and past experience related to the job. You should apply the facts outlined in your résumé to the job to which you're applying. Each cover letter or e-mail should be personalized for the position and company to which you're applying. Don't use "To whom it may concern"; instead, take the time to find out to whom you should actually address the letter. Use "Mr." for male names and "Ms." for female names in your salutation. If you can't figure out the gender of the person who will be handling your application from the name, just use the person's full name ("Dear Jamie Smith"). Finally, end with a complimentary closing, such as "Sincerely, Henry Smith," and be sure to add your signature.

Search the internet for "sample cover letters for internships" or "sample cover letters for high schoolers" to see some good examples. For more advice on cover letters, check out the free guide by Resume Genius at https://resumegenius .com/cover-letters-the-how-to-guide.

Your cover letter or e-mail should be as short as possible while still conveying a sense of who you are and why you want this particular job or to work for this particular company. Do your research into the company and include some details about the company in your letter or e-mail—this demonstrates that you cared enough to take the time to learn something about the company and the job.

Finally, be sure to note all the application preferences of each potential employer, especially when you are applying for a specific position. Some may not want you to include a cover letter at all; others may have specific instructions about formats and what kinds of information they expect you to include. Be sure to follow any of these instructions very closely. It's your first—and maybe only—chance to show the potential employer that you read instructions and follow directions correctly.

RÉSUMÉS, COVER LETTERS, AND ONLINE JOB APPLICATIONS

Résumés and cover letters are holdovers from the era before the internet—even from before personal computers. They were designed to be typed on paper and delivered through the mail. Obviously these days much of the job application process has moved online. Nevertheless, the essential concepts communicated by the résumé and cover letter haven't changed. Most employers who accept online applications either ask that you either e-mail or upload your résumé.

Those who ask you to e-mail your résumé will specify which document formats they accept. The Adobe Acrobat PDF format is often preferred, because many programs can display a PDF (including web browsers), and documents in this format are mostly uneditable—that is, they can't easily be changed. In these cases, you attach the résumé to your e-mail, and your e-mail itself becomes the cover letter. The same principles of the cover letter discussed in this section apply to this e-mail, except you skip the addresses and date at the top and begin directly with the salutation.

Some employers direct you to a section on their website where you can upload your résumé. In these cases, it may not be obvious where your cover letter content should go. Look for a text box labeled something like "Personal Statement" or "Additional Information." Those are good places to add whatever you would normally write in a cover letter. If there doesn't seem to be anywhere like that, see if there is an e-mail link to the hiring manager or whoever will be reading your résumé. Go ahead and send your cover e-mail to this address, mentioning that you have uploaded your résumé (again omitting the addresses and date at the top of your cover letter). Try to use the person's name if it has been given.

The goal of spending so much time and effort crafting a great résumé and cover letter is to achieve one thing: an interview. It's the interview that will determine whether you get the job or not.

Developing Your Interviewing Skills

The best way to avoid nerves and keep calm when you're interviewing is to be prepared. It's okay to feel scared, but keep it in perspective. It's likely that you'll receive many more rejections than acceptances in your professional life, as we all do. However, you only need one "yes" to start out. Think of the interviewing process as a learning experience. With the right attitude, you will learn from each one and get better with each subsequent interview. That should be your overarching goal. Consider these tips and tricks when interviewing, whether it be for a job, internship, recruitment position, or something else entirely:

- Practice interviewing with a friend or relative. Practicing will help calm your nerves and make you feel more prepared. Ask for specific feedback from your friends. Do you need to speak more loudly? Are you making enough eye contact? Are you actively listening when the other person is speaking?

- Learn as much as you can about the company or organization, and be sure to understand the position for which you're applying. This will show the interviewer that you are motivated and interested in the organization.
- Speak up during the interview. Convey to the interviewer important points about yourself. Don't be afraid to ask questions. Try to remember the interviewers' names and call them by name.
- Arrive early and dress professionally and appropriately. (You can read more about proper dress in a following section.)
- Don't show up hungry or thirsty or having to go to the bathroom. Give yourself plenty of time to take care of that before you arrive.
- Take some time to prepare answers to commonly asked questions. Be ready to describe your career or educational goals to the interviewer.[2]

> "To be a good police officer, you need good interpersonal skills and the ability to listen. A full 98 percent of the job is communicating! That's with citizens, suspects, coworkers, and so on. It's essential."—Maureen O'Brien, twenty-seven-year veteran police officer

Common questions you may be asked during a job interview include:

- Tell me about yourself.
- What are your greatest strengths?
- What are your weaknesses?
- Tell me something about yourself that's not on your résumé.
- What are your career goals?
- How do you handle failure? Are you willing to fail?
- How do you handle stress and pressure?
- What are you passionate about?
- Why do you want to work for us?

> Bring a notebook and a pen to the interview. That way you can take some notes, and they'll give you something to do with your hands.

The interview might be with one person or more than one at the same time.

Jot down notes about your answers to these questions, but don't try to memorize the answers. You don't want to come off as too rehearsed during the interview. Remember to be as specific and detailed as possible when answering these questions. Your goal is to set yourself apart in some way from the other interviewees. Always accentuate the positive, even when you're asked about something you did not like, or about failure or stress. Most importantly, though, be yourself.

Active listening is the process of fully concentrating on what is being said, understanding it, and providing nonverbal cues and responses to the person talking.[3] It's the opposite of being distracted and thinking about something else when someone is talking. Active listening takes practice. You might find that your mind wanders and you need to bring it back to the person talking (and this could happen multiple times during one conversation). Practice this technique in regular conversations with friends and relatives. In addition to giving a better interview, it can cut down on nerves and make you more popular with friends and family, as everyone wants to feel that they are really being heard. For more on active listening, check out www.mindtools.com/CommSkll/ActiveListening.htm.

You should also be ready to ask questions of your interviewer. In a practical sense, there should be some questions you have that you can't find the answers to on the website or in the literature. Also, asking questions shows that you are interested and have done your homework. Avoid asking questions about salary or special benefits at this stage, and don't ask about anything negative that you've heard about the company. Keep the questions positive and related to the position to which you're applying. Some example questions to potential employers include:

- What is a typical career path for a person in this position?
- How would you describe the ideal candidate for this position?
- How is the department organized?
- What kind of responsibilities come with this job? (Don't ask this if it has already been addressed in the job description or discussion.)
- What can I do as a follow-up?
- When do you expect to reach a decision?

Remember, it's a good idea to practice interviewing with a friend or relative. At the very least, you should practice by yourself, answering common interview questions. The Balance Careers offers a long list of common questions asked in interviews at www.thebalancecareers.com/job-interview-questions-and-answers-2061204. You could spend quite a while going through those questions and coming up with answers to prepare yourself.

When you're talking to the interviewer, relax. Take your time. Use as much detail as you can when describing your education and experience. Look the interviewer in the eye when you talk.

If you know someone who already works at the company, ask him or her for some inside advice and find out whether it's okay to mention his or her name during the interview. If the interviewer finds out you know someone who works there, that can really work in your favor.

Dressing Appropriately

A job interview means you have to wear a suit and tie, right? Well, if you want to become a bond trader or a lawyer, yes. But probably not if you're interviewing for a job as a first responder. A police chief or EMT director might look at you funny if you showed up dressed to the nines.

What you're looking for here is business casual. This is less formal than business attire (like a suit), but a step up from jeans, a T-shirt, and sneakers:

- *For men:* You can't go wrong with khaki pants, a polo or button-up shirt, and brown or black shoes.
- *For women:* Wear nice slacks, a shirt or blouse that isn't too revealing, and nice flats or shoes with a heel that's not too high.

> You may want to find out in advance whether the organization has a dress code. Don't hesitate to ask the person who's going to interview you if you're unsure what to wear. You can also call the main number and ask the receptionist what people typically wear to interviews.

Even something like "business casual" can be interpreted in many ways, so do some research to find out what exactly is expected of you.

Knowing What Employers Expect

You're almost certainly not the only candidate the employer is interviewing for the position. And if you think about it, they would only have called in people who were qualified for the job. That means that based on education, skills, and experience, all the people who are also interviewing could technically do the job. How, then, will they choose from all the candidates?

According to *Forbes* magazine, employers are looking for twelve qualities in you as an employee, and the interview process is meant to bring out these qualities for evaluation.[4] The employer wants to see that you:

- Work well on a team
- Understand your path
- Know what you want in your career
- Can point to your successes
- Know your strengths
- Think independently
- Like to solve problems
- Have ambition
- Are proactive
- Like learning new things
- Are goal oriented
- Are responsible

Being able to convince an employer that you love to learn new things is one of the best ways to turn yourself into a candidate they won't be able to pass up. One last piece of advice, and in the end this may be the most valuable and crucial of all: Be the kind of person other people like working with. It's sort of the Golden Rule as applied to the workplace.

Following Up

Following up is a delicate procedure that must be handled with a certain amount of thought and care. A good way to think of it is that you want to be on the interviewer's mind but not in his or her face. You don't want to let too many days go by without any communication, but you also don't want to become annoying.

Following up usually takes place over the phone or through e-mail. You want to follow up after these events (unless they contact you first):

- *After sending a résumé/cover letter to a prospective employer:* If you promptly receive an e-mail or phone call acknowledging your correspondence, that's probably good enough for now. You contacted them, and they contacted you to acknowledge it. You're even, and at that point you should give them around a week to contact you again. If they don't within a week, it's appropriate to contact them again (via the same method, phone or e-mail) to inquire about setting up a time to meet to discuss the matter further. This shows you are still interested.

- *After submitting your application:* If you submitted a job application online, you will likely receive a confirmation e-mail right away. If you mailed in your application, you may get a postcard a few days later to acknowledge it—or you may not. In either case, online or through the mail, if you hear nothing for a week, it's generally okay to contact the company again to inquire about it. This shows you're eager for the job.

- *After being invited to an interview:* A quick, short e-mail to thank them for scheduling an interview is appropriate. This is simply to be polite.

- *After an interview:* Immediately after your interview, you *must* go home and compose an e-mail to your interviewer(s) or to your contact at the company who set up the interview (or both—use your own judgment about what is appropriate). Do this as soon as possible, within the hour if you can. In this e-mail you should thank them for their time and for the opportunity to discuss the position. Say you enjoyed meeting them and look forward to talking again. This is also a matter of politeness, and it shows professionalism, respect, and courtesy.

Always read the instructions carefully regarding submitting an application or corresponding with a company. If they spell out rules for contacting them, do not break those rules without a very good reason. Wondering about how they liked your résumé or when you'll be interviewed are not good enough reasons. The only good reason would be that you are no longer interested or available as a candidate (for example, because you just accepted another job).

EFFECTIVELY HANDLING STRESS

As you're forging ahead with your life plans—whether it's training camp, a full-time job, or even a gap year—you might find that these decisions feel very important and heavy and that the stress is difficult to deal with. This is completely normal. Try these simple techniques to relieve stress:

- Take deep breaths in and out. Try this for thirty seconds. You'll be amazed at how it can help.
- Close your eyes and clear your mind.
- Go scream at the passing subway car. Or lock yourself in a closet and scream. Or scream into a pillow. For some people, this can really help.
- Keep the issue in perspective. Any decision you make now can be changed if it doesn't work out.

Want to know how to avoid stress altogether? It is surprisingly simple. Of course, simple doesn't always mean easy, but these ideas are basic and make sense based on what we know about the human body:

- Get enough sleep.
- Eat healthy.
- Get exercise.
- Go outside.
- Schedule downtime.
- Connect with friends and family.

The bottom line is that you need to take time for self-care. There will always be stress in life, but how you deal with it makes all the difference. This only becomes more important as you enter the workforce and maybe have a family. Developing good, consistent habits related to self-care now will serve you all your life.

Beware the social media trap! Prospective employers will check your social media profile, so make sure there is nothing too personal, explicit, or inappropriate out there. When you communicate out to the world on social media, don't use profanity—and be sure to use proper grammar. Think about the version of yourself you are portraying online. Is it favorable or at least neutral to potential employers? They will look, rest assured.

FIREFIGHTING: CHALLENGING, REWARDING, DIFFICULT, AND WORTH IT!

Matt Hahn.
Courtesy of Matt Hahn

Matt Hahn has been a firefighter for the Indianapolis Fire Department for twenty years. He started his career by working as a substitute firefighter for three years, where he filled in for off-duty firefighters, and then made the transition to a full-time assignment. He has done engine work, ladder work, squad work, hazmat, and heavy rescue, tactical. (Heavy rescue, tactical involves rescues of people missing in water, rope rescues below ground, rescuing window washers off of buildings, three-hundred-foot tower rescues, and extraction out of cars in collisions.) He currently serves as the engine lieutenant on IFD Engine 31/B.

Can you explain how you became interested in being a firefighter? How did you get your first position?

I was going to college and paying for it myself, but I didn't know what I wanted to do. I took some time off to soul search. During that time, I saw someone with the words "Fire Department" on their shirt, which sparked my interest. As it turns out, my grandfather, great-grandfather, and great-uncle were all firefighters. I took classes at Ivy Tech University for the fire science degree and volunteered at different departments. I became hooked.

The Indianapolis Fire Department is very competitive and hard to get on. We often have about twenty-five hundred applicants and hire about fifty to sixty people from that pool. If they take you on, you go through their academy, which involves four to five months of training, including EMS and fire science education.

What is a typical day in your job?

The IFD averages three fires a day! We work twenty-four-hour shifts. You relieve your guy—you get your gear on your rig and thoroughly check all of your equipment. Then we all meet in the kitchen and touch base and catch up, do a status, and chat socially. We do our morning housework around the station. We check out and clean up our apparatus and replace what needs replacing. We then work out, cook lunch, and so on. There can be lots of downtime, where you can work on your off-day job if you have one, work out, work on projects, or read. There are often training or classes and building inspections. Get dinner, and everyone helps to make it. Throw six to ten emergency runs in there during that twenty-four-hour period. Restock everything after the runs so all the apparatus is ready for another run. We all have two sets of gear.

What's the best part of being a firefighter?

Helping people is the best, absolutely. That's what drew me in, more even than family tradition and the fire department comradeship. I wanted to do something that made a difference. I am not money motivated as much; I wanted to have a full heart, and helping people does that for me.

I've had eclectic runs, from funny to the worst. You see the best and worst in people. I was going to be either a teacher, a nurse, or a firefighter. I really liked the teamwork and the culture of the firefighters, which is what drew me in. The culture and friendships are amazing.

What's the most challenging part of your job?

The hardest part is the mental strain. It's hard to leave it all at work, for sure. Being diagnosed with PTSD is common for firefighters. I've seen lots of things that I wish I could unsee. You question yourself—could you have done better and why did that happen. You can get cynical. One of the worst is seeing children in harm's way.

Many firefighters don't share their trauma and stress with other firefighters because they don't want to be a liability to their coworkers. You have to process it and talk to someone about it, preferably a professional. Reach out to your division that provides support. You need to talk to someone. Validation from senior firefighters can really help as well.

The schedule gets in the way, too, but that's not as hard to deal with. You will miss birthdays and Christmas mornings sometimes.

Some seventy of our twelve hundred firefighters have suffered from cancer of some kind. With the toxins burning these days, it's much worse than when the main things burning were wood and paper. The smoke even looks different—it's black smoke, and it's full of toxins.

What's the most surprising thing about your job?

It's a physical job. For one, the gear is sixty-five pounds! Also, the variety of runs that you go on is surprising. It's a real diversity of people living in the city of downtown Indianapolis. Every day, you don't know what's going to happen. At the heavy rescue house, you really get unique situations. It's a privilege.

What is your advice for a young person considering this career?

Work toward a fire science degree; network and meet firefighters at the station.

Get into the culture to see if you like it. Don't get sucked into the Hollywood ideas—get a real taste of it. If you're over eighteen, you can ride out with firefighters. Get firsthand experience as much as you can.

Get in good physical shape and do some soul searching.

Keep in mind that you are married to your pension. By their midfifties, most firefighters have to check out—just due to the physicality of the job. But the young guys do take care of the older guys. It's the culture. You will spend a third of your life with them, so make sure the culture fits your personality.

How can a young person prepare for this career while in high school?

Some departments have explorer programs, which are a great opportunity. Visit firehouses and look at going to school for a fire science degree. It's getting more and more important to have a degree. Get good grades.

I can't stress enough having a sound, healthy mind and good coping skills. You need to be safe, and your mind needs to be mentally and spiritually sound. You have to make an effort to confront the ugly issues. Your spouse needs to support and understand you as well.

What's next for you?

I look forward to mentoring other firefighters and growing as a leader. I enjoy being a part of a team. Teamwork is the whole premise of the fire service. You need to draw on others. Teamwork is such a big part of it.

Personal contacts can make the difference! Don't be afraid to contact people you know. Personal connections can be a great way to find jobs and internship opportunities. Your high school teachers, your coaches and mentors, and your friends' parents are all examples of people who very well may know about jobs or internships that would suit you. Start asking several months before you hope to start a job or internship, because it will take some time to do research and arrange interviews. You can also use social media in your search. LinkedIn (www.linkedin.com), for example, includes lots of searchable information on local companies. Follow and interact with people on social media to get their attention. Just remember to act professionally and communicate with proper grammar, just as you would in person.

Summary

Well, you made it to the end of this book! Hopefully, you have learned enough about these fields to start your journey, or to continue along your path. If you've reached the end and you feel like one of these careers is right for you, that's great news. If you've figured out that this isn't the right field for you, that's good information to learn, too. For many of us, figuring out what we *don't* want to do and what we *don't* like is an important step in finding the right career.

With a little hard work and perseverance, you'll be on your way to career success.

There is a lot of good news about a career as a first responder, and it's a very smart career choice for anyone with a passion to help people. It's a great career for people who get energy from working with other people. Job demand is high and will continue to grow. Whether you decide to attend a four-year university, go to community college, or take a gap year, having a plan and an idea about your future can help guide your decisions. After reading this book, you should be well on your way to having a plan for your future. Good luck to you as you move ahead!

Notes

Introduction

1. Bureau of Labor Statistics, United States Department of Labor, "EMTs and Paramedics: Job Outlook," www.bls.gov/ooh/healthcare/emts-and-paramedics.htm#tab-6.
2. Ibid.

Chapter 1

1. CollegeAtlas.org, "Statistics of a College Dropout," www.collegeatlas.org/wp-content/uploads/2014/08/college-dropout-2017.jpg.
2. National Fire Protection Association, "Fire Department Calls," www.nfpa.org/News-and-Research/Data-research-and-tools/Emergency-Responders/Fire-department-calls.
3. Bureau of Labor Statistics, US Department of Labor, "What Firefighters Do," www.bls.gov/ooh/protective-service/firefighters.htm#tab-2.
4. Bureau of Labor Statistics, "Firefighters: Work Environment," www.bls.gov/ooh/protective-service/firefighters.htm#tab-3.
5. Study.com, "Fire Fighter Education Requirements," www.study.com/fire_fighter_education.html.
6. Ben Evards and Gary P. Stein, "US Fire Department Profile," National Fire Protection Association, March 2019, www.nfpa.org/News-and-Research/Data-research-and-tools/Emergency-Responders/US-fire-department-profile.
7. National Institute for Occupational Safety and Health, "NIOSH Study of Firefighters Finds Increased Rates of Cancer," press release, October 17, 2013, http://www.cdc.gov/niosh/updates/upd-10-17-13.html.
8. Madeline Bodin, "Volunteer Fire Departments Are Struggling to Retain Firefighters, While 911 Calls Are Surging," *Government Technology*, June 29, 2017, www.govtech.com/em/disaster/EM-Summer-2017-Dwindling-Force.html.

9. Bureau of Labor Statistics, US Department of Labor, "Firefighters," www
.bls.gov/ooh/protective-service/firefighters.htm.

10. Bureau of Labor Statistics, US Department of Labor, "What Police and
Detectives Do," www.bls.gov/ooh/protective-service/police-and-detectives.htm#tab-2.

11. Bureau of Labor Statistics, US Department of Labor, "Police and Detectives,"
www.bls.gov/ooh/protective-service/police-and-detectives.htm.

12. Bureau of Labor Statistics, US Department of Labor "What EMTs and
Paramedics Do," www.bls.gov/ooh/healthcare/emts-and-paramedics.htm#tab-2.

13. Unitek EMT, "The Difference between EMT Certification Levels," September
13, 2013, www.unitekemt.com/articles/the-difference-between-emt-certification-levels.

14. Bureau of Labor Statistics, "What EMTs and Paramedics Do."

15. Bureau of Labor Statistics, US Department of Labor, "EMTs and Paramedics,"
www.bls.gov/ooh/healthcare/emts-and-paramedics.htm.

16. Unitek EMT, "The Difference between EMT Certification Levels."

17. Ibid.

18. Bureau of Labor Statistics, "EMTs and Paramedics."

Chapter 2

1. Study.com, "Fire Fighter Education Requirements," www.study.com/fire
_fighter_education.html.

2. Ibid.

3. Unitek EMT, "The Difference between EMT Certification Levels," September
13, 2013, www.unitekemt.com/articles/the-difference-between-emt-certification-levels.

4. Ibid.

5. Ibid.

6. Ibid.

Chapter 3

1. Peter Van Buskirk, "Finding a Good College Fit," *U.S. News & World
Report*, June 13, 2011, www.usnews.com/education/blogs/the-college-admissions
-insider/2011/06/13/finding-a-good-college-fit.

2. National Center for Education Statistics, "Fast Facts: Graduation Rates,"
https://nces.ed.gov/fastfacts/display.asp?id=40.

3. US Department of Education, "Focusing Higher Education on Student Success," July 27, 2015, www.ed.gov/news/press-releases/fact-sheet-focusing-higher-education-student-success.

4. Study.com, "Fire Fighter Education Requirements," www.study.com/fire_fighter_education.html.

5. Discover Policing, "Basic Requirements," www.discoverpolicing.org/about-policing/basic-requirements.

6. Unitek EMT, "The Difference between EMT Certification Levels," www.unitekemt.com/articles/the-difference-between-emt-certification-levels.

7. College Board, "How Much Is Tuition?" https://parents.collegeboard.org/faq/how-much-tuition.

8. Johanna Sorrentino, "How Much Does Trade School Costs?" *Real Work Matters*, June 14, 2016, www.rwm.org/articles/how-much-does-trade-school-cost.

9. College Board, "Understanding College Costs," https://bigfuture.collegeboard.org/pay-for-college/college-costs/understanding-college-costs.

10. Gap Year Association, "Research Statement," https://www.gapyearassociation.org/assets/2015%20NAS%20Report.pdf.

11. Federal Student Aid, US Department of Education, "FAFSA Changes for 2017–2018," https://studentaid.ed.gov/sa/announcements.

Chapter 4

1. The Ladders, "Keeping an Eye on Recruiter Behavior," https://cdn.theladders.net/static/images/basicSite/pdfs/TheLadders-EyeTracking-StudyC2. pdf.

2. Justin Ross Muchnick, *Teens' Guide to College & Career Planning*, 12th ed. (Lawrenceville, NJ: Peterson's, 2015), 179–80.

3. Mind Tools, "Active Listening: Hear What People Are Really Saying," www.mindtools.com/CommSkll/ActiveListening.htm.

4. Liz Ryan, "12 Qualities Employers Look for When They're Hiring," *Forbes*, March 2, 2016, www.forbes.com/sites/lizryan/2016/03/02/12-qualities-employers-look-for-when-theyre-hiring/#8ba06d22c242.

Glossary

accreditation: The act of officially recognizing an organizational body, person, or educational facility as having a particular status or being qualified to perform a particular activity. For example, schools and colleges are accredited. *See also* certification.

ACT: One of the standardized college entrance tests that anyone wanting to enter undergraduate studies in the United States should take. It measures knowledge and skills in mathematics, English, reading, and science reasoning as they apply to college readiness. There are four multiple-choice sections and an optional writing test. The total score of the ACT is 36. *See also* SAT.

active listening: The process of fully concentrating on what is being said, understanding it, and providing nonverbal cues and responses to the person talking. It's the opposite of being distracted and thinking about something else when someone is talking to you.

associate's degree: A degree awarded by a community or junior college that typically requires two years of study.

baby boomers: The American generation that was born immediately after World War II, from about 1945 until about 1964. During this time, there was a "boom" (large increase) in the number of births in the United States.

bachelor's degree: An undergraduate degree awarded by a college or university that is typically a four-year course of study when pursued full-time, but this can vary by the degree earned and by the university awarding the degree.

cardiopulmonary resuscitation (CPR): Treatment given by a certified professional to a person who has collapsed, has no discernable pulse, and has stopped breathing. It involves giving the victim external cardiac massage and breaths into the lungs in order to restore oxygen intake and blood circulation.

cardiovascular system: The system of the human body making up the heart and blood, including veins and arteries. Applicable diseases include stroke, heart attack, and high blood pressure.

certification: The action or process of confirming that an individual has acquired certain skills or knowledge, usually provided by some third-party review, assessment, or educational body. Individuals, not organizations, are certified. *See also* accreditation.

detective unit: A unit of police officers who gather facts and collect evidence for criminal cases, conducting interviews, examining records, observing the activities of suspects, and participating in raids and arrests. Detectives usually specialize in investigating one type of crime, such as homicide or fraud. They can be uniformed or plainclothes investigators.

diagnosis: When a healthcare professional determines the nature of an illness or problem after examining a patient.

emergency medical responder (EMR): A first responder trained to provide basic medical care with minimal equipment. These workers may provide immediate lifesaving interventions while waiting for other EMS resources to arrive. Jobs in this category are also called emergency care attendants, certified first responders, or similar.

emergency medical technician (EMT): First responders who work in the emergency medical service (EMS) profession. They are specifically trained and certified to treat the sick and injured in emergency situations, responding to emergency 911 calls by performing medical services as they are transporting patients to medical facilities. There are three levels of EMT certification: EMT-Basic, EMT-Intermediate, and EMT-Paramedic.

fire science: The study of the causes, effects, and prevention of fire using the rules of science and engineering. Firefighting, fire safety, fire protection, and fire prevention are the main areas of study in fire science. In addition, fire science studies fire management, fire behavior, fire investigation, and hazardous materials. Fire science degree and certificate programs are offered across the country.

Kelly shift schedule: Many firefighters work some version of this schedule, which involves working three twenty-four-hour shifts on alternate days, followed by four consecutive days off. You might work on Wednesday, Friday, and Sunday, and then have the next four days off. This type of schedule rotates, so you would then work twenty-four-hour shifts on Friday, Sunday, and Tuesday, and then be off the next four days.

gap year: A year between high school and college (or sometimes between college and postgraduate studies) during which the student is not in school but is instead involved in other pursuits, typically volunteer programs such as the Peace Corps, in travel experiences, or in work and teaching experiences.

grants: Money to pay for postsecondary education that is typically awarded to students who have financial need, but can also be used in the areas of athletics, academics, demographics, veteran support, and special talents. Grants do not have to be paid back.

internal affairs unit: A unit of police officers who investigate and unearth what really occurred when an officer or department is accused of misconduct. These officers typically work outside of the traditional command structure.

master's degree: A postgraduate degree awarded by colleges and universities that requires at least one additional year of study after obtaining a bachelor's degree. The degree holder shows mastery of a specific field.

paramedic: An EMT with the highest level of certification. Paramedics are certified to perform more advanced medical procedures on their patients, including administering medications orally and intravenously, starting intravenous lines, providing advanced airway management for patients, interpreting electrocardiograms (EKGs), and learning to resuscitate and support patients with significant health problems such as heart attacks and traumas.

personal statement: A written description of your accomplishments, outlook, interests, goals, and personality that is an important part of your college application. The personal statement should set you apart from other applicants. The required length depends on the institution, but they generally range from one to two pages, or five hundred to one thousand words.

postsecondary degree: An educational degree above and beyond a high school education. This is a general description that includes trade certificates and certifications; associate's, bachelor's degrees, and master's degrees; and beyond.

post-traumatic stress disorder (PTSD): An anxiety disorder that can be the result of experiencing a traumatic event. People suffering from PTSD may have intense fear, helplessness, guilt, and stress, long after the traumatic event is over, often reliving these events in their minds and suffering from flashbacks. Many first responders struggle with bouts of PTSD due to the traumatic nature of their jobs.

SAT: One of the standardized tests in the United States that anyone applying to undergraduate studies should take. It measures verbal and mathematical reasoning abilities as they relate to predicting successful performance in college. It is intended to complement a student's GPA and school record in assessing readiness for college. The total score of the SAT is 1600. *See also* ACT.

scholarships: Merit-based aid used to pay for postsecondary education that does not have to be paid back. Scholarships are typically awarded based on academic excellence or some other special talent, such as music or art.

SWAT unit: An elite unit within a police force that is used in exceptional crisis situations that require increased firepower or special tactics, often dealing, for example, with hostage and terrorist situations. SWAT stands for *Special Weapons and Tactics.*

vice unit: A unit of police officers who focus on crime related to narcotics, alcohol, gambling, and prostitution. These officers sometimes go undercover to investigate potential illegal operations.

Resources

Are you looking for more information about the fields within the first responder umbrella, which in this book include firefighters, police officers, EMTs, and paramedics? Do you want to know more about the application process for college or training, or need some help finding the right educational/vocational fit for you? Do you want a quick way to search for a good college or school? Try these resources as a starting point on your journey toward finding a great career!

Books

Fiske, Edward. *Fiske Guide to Colleges*. Naperville, IL: Sourcebooks, 2018.

Gilmartin, Kevin M. *Emotional Survival for Law Enforcement: A Guide for Officers and Their Families*. Tucson, AZ: E-S Press, 2002.

Kerrigan, Dan, and Jim Moss. *Firefighter Functional Fitness: The Essential Guide to Optimal Firefighter Performance and Longevity*. N.p.: Firefighter Toolbox, 2016.

Le Baudour, Chris, and J. David Bergeron. *Emergency Medical Responder: First on Scene*, 10th ed. Hoboken, NJ: Pearson, 2015.

Muchnick, Justin Ross. *Teens' Guide to College & Career Planning*, 12th ed. Lawrenceville, NJ: Peterson's, 2015.

Princeton Review. *The Best 382 Colleges, 2018 Edition: Everything You Need to Make the Right College Choice*. New York: Princeton Review, 2018.

Strock, James. *Serve to Lead 2.0: Twenty-First Century Leaders Manual*, 2nd ed. N.p.: Serve to Lead Group, 2018.

Titus, Alfred S., Jr. *The Personal Side of Policing: An In-Depth Look at How a Career in Law Enforcement Can Change and Affect Your Life*. Middletown, DE: A. Titus Consulting, 2018.

Websites

American Gap Year Association

www.gapyearassociation.org

The American Gap Year Association's mission is "making transformative gap years an accessible option for all high school graduates." A gap year is a year taken between high school and college to travel, teach, work, volunteer, generally mature, and otherwise experience the world. The website has lots of advice and resources for anyone considering taking a gap year.

The Balance

www.thebalance.com

This site is all about managing money and finances, but also has a large section called Your Career, which provides advice for writing résumés and cover letters, interviewing, and more. Search the site for teens and you can find teen-specific advice and tips.

The College Entrance Examination Board

www.collegeboard.org

The College Entrance Examination Board tracks and summarizes financial data from colleges and universities all over the United States. This great, well-organized site can be your one-stop shop for all things college research. It contains lots of advice and information about taking and doing well on the SAT and ACT, many articles on college planning, a robust college search feature, a scholarship search feature, and a major and career search area. You can type your career of interest (for example, firefighter) into the search box and get back a full page that describes the career; gives advice on how to prepare, where to get experience, and how to pay for it; describes the characteristics you should have to excel in this career; lists helpful classes to take while in high school; and lots of links for more information.

College Grad Career Profiles

www.collegegrad.com/careers

Although this site is primarily geared toward college graduates, the careers profiles area, indicated above, has a list of links to nearly every career you could ever think of. A single click takes you to a very detailed, helpful section that describes the job in detail, explains the educational requirements, includes links to good colleges that offer this career and to actual open jobs and internships, describes the licensing requirements (if any), lists salaries, and much more.

Everyday EMS Tips
www.everydayemstips.com
This site includes lots of short posts that are packed with information. The blog posts are written by guest authors who are EMS professionals or EMS students, which makes for current and relatable content. The site includes a little bit of everything, from EMS tips, reviews, and podcasts, to videos and case studies.

Firefighter Toolbox
www.firefightertoolbox.com
With a mission to build better firefighters and leaders, this site includes product reviews, health and fitness tips, a podcast, and articles covering all aspects of being a firefighter.

Firehouse
www.firehouse.com
This site is a great resource for breaking news, podcasts, blogs, webcasts, and information on firefighting, training, jobs, technical rescue, and more.

Journal of Emergency Medical Services (JEMS) Editor Blog
www.jemseditorblog.com
JEMS editor in chief A. J. Heightman has more than thirty years of EMS experience, which makes for an excellent blog. He posts a couple of times a month, and the visuals and content are well worth the wait. His posts are typically short, but engaging and thought provoking.

Khan Academy
www.khanacademy.org
The Khan Academy website is an impressive collection of articles, courses, and videos about many educational topics in math, science, and the humanities. You can search any topic or subject (by subject matter and grade), and read lessons, take courses, and watch videos to learn all about it. The site includes test prep information for the SAT, ACT, AP, GMAT, and other standardized tests.

There is also a College Admissions tab with lots of good articles and information, provided in the approachable Khan style.

Law Officer
www.lawofficer.com
This site provides law enforcement with daily breaking news stories as well as editorials about tactics, technology, and training officers need to stay safe on the job.

Life under the Lights
www.lifeunderthelights.com
This is a great site for those interested in EMS who want to get a realistic view of this profession. The writer, Chris Kaiser, is an EMS professional and a firefighter, and his goal is to shed light on the professional life of EMTs. His blog centers around breaking the stereotypes of EMS professionals and spreading awareness of the high-demand job for what it really is.

Live Career
www.livecareer.com
This site has an impressive number of resources directed toward teens for writing résumés and cover letters, as well as interviewing.

Mapping Your Future
www.mappingyourfuture.org
This site helps young people figure out what they want to do and maps out how to reach career goals. Includes helpful tips on résumé writing, job hunting, job interviewing, and more.

Monster.com
www.monster.com
This is perhaps the most well-known and certainly one of the largest employment websites in the United States. You fill in a couple of search boxes and away you go. You can sort by job title, of course, as well as by company name, location, salary range, experience range, and much more. The site also includes information about career fairs, advice on résumés and interviewing, and more.

National Fire Protection Association
www.nfpa.org
Called "the leading information and knowledge resource on fire, electrical, and related hazards," the NFPA's website includes loads of information pertaining to fire safety and prevention, including training, public education, news and research, and code and standards data.

Occupational Outlook Handbook
www.bls.gov/ooh
The US Bureau of Labor Statistics produces this website, which offers lots of relevant and updated information about various careers, including average salaries, how to work in the industry, job market outlook, typical work environments, and what workers do on the job. See www.bls.gov/emp for a full list of employment projections.

Peterson's College Prep
www.petersons.com
In addition to lots of information about preparing for the ACT and SAT and easily searchable information about scholarships nationwide, the Peterson's site includes a comprehensive search feature for universities and schools based on location, major, name, and more.

PoliceOne
www.policeone.com
Dubbed "the one resource for police officers and law enforcement," this site includes news from all over the country, training advice, and videos of all things related to law enforcement. On this site, you can find breaking news, product reviews, job postings, and more.

POLICE Magazine
www.policemag.com
This website is dedicated to providing law enforcement officers of all ranks with information that will help them do their jobs more efficiently, professionally, and safely. Each issue of *POLICE* includes columns written by current and retired police, firearms, and legal experts, as well as topical issue-oriented features produced by leading law enforcement journalists.

Study.com
www.study.com
Similar to Khan Academy, Study.com allows you to search any topic or subject and read lessons, take courses, and watch videos to learn all about it.

TeenLife
www.teenlife.com
This site calls itself "the leading source for college preparation," and it includes lots of information about summer programs, gap year programs, community service, and more. Promoting the belief that spending time out "in the world" outside of the classroom can help students develop important life skills, this site contains lots of links to volunteer and summer programs.

U.S. News & World Report *College Rankings*
www.usnews.com/best-colleges
U.S. News & World Report provides almost fifty different types of numerical rankings and lists of colleges throughout the United States to help students with their college search. You can search colleges by best reviewed, best value for the money, best liberal arts schools, best schools for B students, and more.

About the Author

Kezia Endsley is an editor and author from Indianapolis, Indiana. In addition to editing technical publications and writing books for teens, she enjoys running and triathlons, traveling, reading, and spending time with her family and many pets.

EDITORIAL BOARD